ON

SARTRE

Richard Kamber
The College of New Jersey

Wadsworth
Thomson Learning..

Australia • Canada • Mexico • Singapore • Spain
United Kingdom • United States

To Leah, Ann, and Kerin

Printed in the United States of America
2 3 4 5 6 7 03 02 01 00

For permission to use material from this text, contact us:
Web: http://www.thomsonrights.com
Fax: 1-800-730-2215
Phone: 1-800-730-2214

For more information, contact:
Wadsworth/Thomson Learning, Inc.
10 Davis Drive
Belmont, CA 94002-3098
USA
http://www.wadsworth.com

ISBN: 0-534-57624-9

CONTENTS

PREFACE

I have written *On Sartre* to provide a clear, accurate, and interesting overview of Jean-Paul Sartre's life and work as a philosopher. Although this book may be of interest to some scholars, it is intended primarily as a guide for readers who want to understand the essentials of Sartre's philosophy but lack a substantial background in philosophy. Consequently, I have designed this book so that it presupposes only a willingness to read, think, and learn. Since *On Sartre* is a short book, I have emphasized those elements in Sartre's philosophy which I believe are most original and most likely to endure. For example, I spend far more time on Sartre's work as an existentialist and phenomenologist, than on his work as a Marxist. (These terms will be explained in due course.)

Chapter 1 of this book deals with preliminary matters that are helpful to cover before getting into the details of Sartre's life and work. Chapter 2 is a compact but reasonably comprehensive biography, with particular attention to Sartre's philosophical development. It is a useful introduction to who Sartre was and what he did. The remaining chapters are devoted to the examination and evaluation of selected philosophical views and arguments. My strategy in those chapters is to connect some of Sartre's most memorable work as a philosopher to perennial problems in Western philosophy. In each of these chapters, I offer a brief explanation of the problems and proposed solutions which form the philosophical background for Sartre's views and arguments. My purpose is to help make clear, not only what Sartre said, but also why he said it and to what extent it succeeds as philosophy.

1
Jean-Paul Sartre: Philosopher

A. Jean-Paul Sartre: Philosopher

Although much of Sartre's life and many of his works belonged to the spheres of literature or political thought as much as to philosophy, I believe the title 'philosopher' remains especially appropriate for Jean-Paul Sartre. Over the course of his adult life, he practiced philosophy by seeking to understand the world and the human condition at the deepest levels possible. As a seeker of wisdom, Sartre was not afraid to change his mind or strike out in new directions. He liked to say: "I think against myself." He was always more interested in the book he was writing than in the books he had already written. He was always hopeful that his newest insights would be his best.

For the general public, Sartre remains one of the "best known" philosophers of the 20th century. Although relatively few people are familiar with the specific ideas and arguments that make up his philosophy, a good many people have read one or more of his plays, stories, novels, or essays. A substantially larger group can claim familiarity with his name and his connection to existentialism, and, perhaps, his relationship with Simone de Beauvoir. Moreover, some of Sartre's ideas about free will, responsibility, and the necessity of inventing one's own values in a world without God have worked their

1

way into popular culture. For example, Woody Allen's 1989 film, *Crimes and Misdemeanors*, is a brilliant, funny, and remarkably faithful translation of Sartre's ideas into a contemporary murder story. Hence, some people who have never read any of his works may be influenced, nonetheless, by Sartrean ideas that have trickled down to them from other sources.

Among professional philosophers, however, Sartre's reputation has not fared so well. Although he is still recognized as one of the distinctive philosophical figures of the 20th century, there is no school or movement in philosophy today built on his ideas. Most of what is written about Sartre today is historical or biographical. Unlike past philosophers whose views continue to be actively debated in contemporary philosophical discussions, Sartre seems to have been shelved among the honorable mentions in the history of philosophy.

I believe that most professional philosophers have neglected Sartre's work for two reasons in particular. The first is the perception that he had very few original ideas about the nature, limits, or proper uses of philosophy—a tremendously important subject for 20th century philosophy. The second is the assumption that he developed little in the way of original and persuasive strategies for dealing with philosophical problems. In my opinion, the first reason is correct. In contrast to such 20th century philosophical icons as Martin Heidegger (1889-1876) and Ludwig Wittgenstein (1889-1951), Sartre did little to call into question the way in which philosophy is done or to exemplify in his work a radically different way of doing it. Sartre cared more about the adequacy of individual arguments than the adequacy of their methodological foundations. In constructing his own positions, he generally used whatever methods served his needs at the time. However, I believe that the second reason is incorrect. I am convinced that Sartre developed many original and persuasive strategies for dealing with philosophical problems, especially with problems concerning perception and reality, the nature of consciousness, and free will. One purpose of this book is show that this is so.

B. Simone de Beauvoir and Existentialism

The name 'Jean-Paul Sartre' is closely connected with two other names: 'Simone de Beauvoir' and 'existentialism.' Before considering the full story of Sartre's life and works, it is helpful to get clear on Sartre's unique connections with Simone de Beauvoir and existentialism.

Simone de Beauvoir was Sartre's closest friend and confidante for fifty years. They met in the summer of 1929 at the University of Paris, where both were preparing for the *agrégation* (doctoral level) examinations in philosophy. He was twenty-three, she was twenty-one. When grades were announced, Sartre, who had failed the written exam the previous year, was first; Beauvoir was second. They became lovers and remained intimate for several years, but that did not last. What did last was their practice of telling each other about (nearly) everything and their enjoyment of traveling and working together. Sartre, who wrote very rapidly (about twenty pages a day) and often quite carelessly, relied on Beauvoir to read his drafts and suggest changes. Usually, he took her advice. When not together, Sartre and Beauvoir exchanged letters. These letters and Beauvoir's elegant autobiographical works provide a wealth of insight and information about their lives and work.

Who influenced whom? Although Beauvoir insisted that she, unlike Sartre, was not an original and systematic philosopher and that she followed Sartre's philosophical lead, her view has been questioned by a number of feminist scholars. For example, Kate and Edward Fullbrook have argued that Sartre stole most of the ideas in *Being and Nothingness* from early drafts of Beauvoir's first novel *She Came to Stay* (1943). According to the the Fullbrooks, this novel "articulates a philosophical system that in its basic structure differs not at all from the one found in *Being and Nothingness*" (Fullbrook and Fullbrook 1994, 101). They describe this appropriation of Beauvoir's ideas as a "crime" and claim that Sartre and Beauvoir collaborated in covering up this crime. There are many things wrong with the Fullbrooks' argument. First, they do not seem to know much about Sartre's philosophical ideas in *Being and Nothingness* or the development of those ideas during the 1930s. Second, they do not seem to understand the difference between the capacity of literature to suggest philosophical ideas and the capacity of philosophical prose to explain and argue for philosophical ideas. For example, they discover "a densely-packed revision of classical and modern philosophical positions" in the following sentence from *She Came to Stay*: "I am here, my heart is beating" (Fullbrook and Fullbrook 1994, 102). Third, they assume that because Sartre and Beauvoir chose not to make public some of the intimate details of their private lives that they also lied relentlessly about their intellectual collaboration.

Far more convincingly, Margaret Simons has argued for Beauvoir's philosophical originality by demonstrating that the student diary Beauvoir wrote in 1927, two years before meeting Sartre, displays interest in some of the same philosophical issues that Sartre would later address. Simons also points out that Beauvoir's treatments of these issues in 1927 are different in important respects from the treatments Sartre would later develop. (See: Simons 1999, 185-233). Once Sartre and Beauvoir began their intellectual partnership, differences between their views became more difficult to detect. Nevertheless, the pattern of common issues but subtly different treatments persisted over the years. In the 1940s, for example, both Sartre and Beauvoir worked on the problem of "the Other" (conscious interactions between one's own self and other selves) but with divergent emphases. Ultimately, it was Beauvoir's concept of the socially constructed Other that proved more influential.

Although scholars may debate the details, there is no reason to doubt that Sartre borrowed ideas from Beauvoir just as she borrowed ideas from him. Sartre was in fact a great borrower. Throughout his career, he borrowed ideas from many sources. In his early years, he borrowed key ideas from the French rationalist, René Descartes (1596-1650), the German idealist, G. W. F. Hegel (1770-1831), the founder of phenomenology, Edmund Husserl (1859-1938), and the existential philosopher, Martin Heidegger (1889-1976). Later, he borrowed ethical ideas from the great Enlightenment philosopher, Immanuel Kant (1724-1804), and for a time he subordinated his own philosophy to the ideas of Karl Marx (1818-1883), the founder of Communism. Sartre's originality as a philosopher consisted mainly in his creation of new syntheses in which borrowed ideas were profoundly reinterpreted and offered as solutions to traditional philosophical problems. Beauvoir understood this completely. She said: "For me, a philosopher is someone like Spinoza, Hegel, or like Sartre: someone who builds a great system, and not simply someone who loves philosophy . . . and can use in it essays, etc., but it is someone who *truly* constructs a philosophy. And that I did not do" (Simons 1999, 11).

How were Sartre and Beauvoir connected to existentialism? Although the idea of *existential* philosophy—a philosophy focused on *human existence*—was first developed by the Danish philosopher Søren Kierkegaard in the middle of the 19th century, it was not until 1929 that the idea of existentialism as a distinct trend or movement in modern thought first emerged (See: Heinemann 1958, 1-3, 84-93). According to Beauvoir, the French word *'existentialiste'* was coined by the Roman Catholic philosopher Gabriel Marcel, but she and Sartre were very surprised when the word was applied to them (Beauvoir 1966, 433). At first they resisted being labeled existentialists, but by the fall of 1945

4

they embraced '*existentialisme*' as a banner for their own philosophy (Beauvoir 1964, 38). What is existentialism? The word 'existentialism' is most often used today as a covering term for a number of well-known post-1830 European thinkers who focused on issues of human existence, choice, and individual responsibility. Typically, these thinkers take as their point of departure the concrete individual struggling to make sense out of his or her own life. They emphasize that as human beings, we find ourselves thrown into a world we did not make, born to parents we did not choose, and compelled to deal with the challenges of the human condition—such as the anguish of choice, the uncertainty of knowledge, and the inevitability of death. Who were these thinkers? I would say that the central figures of existentialism are:

- Søren Kierkegaard (1813-1855)
- Friedrich Nietzsche (1844-1900)
- Karl Jaspers (1883-1969)
- Gabriel Marcel (1889-1973)
- Martin Heidegger (1889-1976)
- Jean-Paul Sartre (1905-1980)
- Simone de Beauvoir (1908-1986)
- Maurice Merleau-Ponty (1908-1961)
- Albert Camus (1913-1960)

Even with these figures in mind, it is difficult to generalize about existentialism. In fact, it is difficult precisely because these figures disagreed with one another on so many basic issues. Some, like Kierkegaard, Marcel, and Jaspers were deeply religious. Others, like Nietzsche, Sartre, Beauvoir, and Camus, were atheists. Some were political liberals or leftists, others deeply conservative. Martin Heidegger was a member of the Nazi Party. Most championed free will as essential to choice and responsibility, but Nietzsche rejected free will, saying that it was not a question of free or unfree wills but of strong wills and weak wills. Furthermore, two of the best-known figures associated with existentialism, Heidegger and Camus consistently refused to be called existentialists.

In the final analysis, it is Sartre and Beauvoir to whom the label of existentialism remains most firmly attached. In 1945, Sartre declared that the common and defining belief of existentialism is the belief that in the case of human beings "*existence* comes before *essence*" (Sartre, EH 1989, 348). A human being, he explained, is not born with a fixed character or nature; a human being creates his or her own character through choice and action, and, therefore, bears full responsibility for

5

what he or she becomes. Sartre and Beauvoir continued to identify themselves as existentialists well into the 1960s, and Sartre sometimes used the word 'existentialism' as a label for his own brand of existentialism. In 1963, Jaspers, who had played a major role in the formation of 20th century existentialism, said of Sartre:

> I have gained the greatest respect for Sartre. He is not only a thinker and an analyst of phenomena; he has gained an unusually wide audience for this philosophy thanks to his creative writing . . . There is no existentialism. There is Sartre (Suhl 1970, 272).

In the chapters that follow, I say a good deal more about existentialism. Some of it will be comparative, but all of it will be tied to particular figures in the existential movement. The real interest and value of existentialism resides in the lives and works of its individual thinkers rather than in generalizations about existentialism as a whole.

Why is it important to know something about Sartre's life in order to understand his philosophy? More than most philosophers, existentialists tend to see close connections between how an individual lives his or her life with what that individual believes philosophically. Nietzsche, for example, declared that "every great philosophy so far" has been "the personal confession of its author and a kind of involuntary and unconscious memoir" (Nietzsche 1989, 13). Other existentialists do not go as far as Nietzsche, but they do regard the details of a philosopher's life as a source and a test of his or her ideas. Also, like Nietzsche, they believe that what threatens a philosophy is not the connection between life and thought, but failure to acknowledge the connection. For existentialists, the personal is philosophical.

6

2
Life and Works

A. Sartre's Childhood and Education: 1905-1929

Jean-Paul Charles Aymard Sartre was born in Paris on June 21, 1905. His father, Jean-Baptiste Sartre, was an officer in the French navy. His mother, Anne-Marie (née Schweitzer) was the youngest child of a family from Alsace who had moved to France after the Franco-Prussian War to avoid living under German rule. Her first cousin was Albert Schweitzer, who later become famous as a missionary in Africa. When Sartre was fifteen months old his father died of an intestinal disease he contracted in the French colony of Cochin China (now part of Vietnam). As a result, Sartre never knew his father. Lacking any opportunity to support herself, Anne-Marie returned to her parents' home, where she and her son shared "the children's room." Although Sartre and his mother were very close, their relationship in the Schweitzer household was rather like that of an older sister and little brother. Anne-Marie's mother, Louise, ran the house and her father, Charles, ran the family.

According to Sartre, the ten years he spent in the Schweitzer household, first at Meudon and then in Paris, shaped the ambitions that

7

would drive him for the rest of his life. Both of his grandparents were readers, and their rooms were full of books. Charles Schweitzer was a teacher of languages, still handsome, energetic, and sexually profligate at age sixty-five with a long white beard that made him look like traditional pictures of God the Father. Having quarreled with his own sons, Charles was delighted to have a grandson to himself, a child whose character he could mold. He took charge of Sartre's education and encouraged the boy to develop a love for good literature. He warned him not to become a writer—an unreliable profession, but to make a career as a teacher and scholar.

In the meantime, Sartre's mother bought him picture books and adventure stories in order to ensure that her son could enjoy his childhood. But, children, as Sartre would later emphasize, are never merely passive recipients of adult influence. Searching for his own identity, young Sartre was torn between allegiance to his grandfather's high literary values and dreams of being a man of action, a knight errant who would rescue damsels in distress and battle the forces of evil. Between the ages of eight and twelve, Sartre decided to become a writer, or, more precisely, he convinced himself that he was destined to become a writer. Here was a destiny that would allow him to justify his existence by becoming indispensable to the world of letters. He would be a hero, but the weapon of his heroism would be a pen not a sword. (Significantly, perhaps, Sartre always preferred a pen to a typewriter.)

In 1917, Sartre's mother remarried. Her new husband was Joseph Mancy, a former admirer, who was now a prosperous engineer, managing shipbuilding yards in La Rochelle. The next three years were among the unhappiest in Sartre's life. He disliked being in La Rochelle and resented his stepfather. Although Mancy was generous with Sartre, the boy despised his authoritarian manner and middle-class values. Neither did Sartre appreciate his stepfather's efforts to tutor him in science and mathematics. Perhaps, most of all, Sartre resented having to share the affections of his mother with an intruder. In school, he had difficulty making friends. He fought with his classmates, and then tried to buy their friendship with pastries he purchased by selling books from his home and stealing money from his mother's handbag. He was caught and knew the shame of being treated as a thief. When his grandfather dropped a coin in a store he stooped in pain to pick it up rather than let his dishonest grandson retrieve it.

Although Sartre had been raised as a Catholic, religion had never gripped his soul with any notable force. At about this time, he suddenly discovered that he no longer believed in God.

In 1920, his grandfather arranged for him to attend school in Paris

8

at the distinguished *Lycée Henri IV.* (In the French system of education, a *lycée* provided preparation for university studies. A student entered at age twelve and graduated at nineteen.) There, Sartre came under the influence of a talented and iconoclastic philosopher who called himself Alain (Emile Auguste Chartier). There too, he formed his first close friendship, with a student named Paul Nizan. Despite truancy and rebelliousness, Sartre did well in school. Sartre's greatest gift was what he would later call his "golden brain." The rest of his body was another matter. Like his father, Sartre was short. As a young man, his height was just five foot two. But unlike either of his parents, he was ugly. At the age of four, he caught a cold at the beach, which led to near-blindness in his right eye and loss of muscular control. Later, his face was disfigured by acne that left pockmarks and bloated features. Short and stocky, walleyed, and pockmarked, Sartre described himself as a "toad." To compensate for his appearance, he developed his muscles, took boxing lessons, and cultivated a remarkably engaging personality. He had an impressive voice, a good sense of humor, and an astonishing capacity for conversation. Despite his ugliness, he managed to have long-term sexual relationships with many attractive women.

In 1924, he was admitted to the exclusive L'Ecole Normale Supérieure (ENS) to prepare for a university degree. The ENS provided complementary instruction to the regular course of studies at the Sorbonne, but Sartre seldom went to the Sorbonne. Most of what Sartre learned during his five years of university studies he learned from books and conversations with other students. Luckily, there were brilliant students taking a degree in Paris at that time. Among them were Simone Weil, Raymond Aron, Maurice Merleau-Ponty, Jean Hyppolite, and Simone de Beauvoir. Sartre's closest friends were Paul Nizan and René Maheu. It was Maheu, who may have been Beauvoir's first lover, who gave her her nickname. He called her "the Beaver" (*le Castor*) because she enjoyed company and worked so constructively. As mentioned above, Sartre failed the written examination for the *agégation* in 1928, but ranked in first place in 1929.

B. Soldier, Teacher, Philosopher, and Writer: 1930-1938

Although Sartre left the university eager to fulfill his destiny as a writer, nearly seven years would pass before his first book was published. In spite of partial blindness, he was required by French law to complete eighteen months of military training. Stationed at Fort Saint Cyr in November 1924, he was trained as an army meteorologist, and for the first time in his adult life, experienced the boredom of days that repeated themselves without change. In April, 1931 he began a teaching appointment at a *lycée* in Le Havre, a commercial seaport in northeastern France. He soon became popular with students, who enjoyed his casual manners and style of teaching. While other teachers took care to maintain "the proper distance" between themselves and students, he made a practice of socializing with students. He ate with them, drank with them, played Ping-Pong with them, and joined their picnics. At the end of one term, he went drinking with a group of students, and they ended up in whorehouse. This episode gave him an enduring reputation at the lycée. On the other hand, he found Le Havre to be a dull, dreary, and provincial town. He particularly disliked the smug self-righteousness of its civic leaders and prominent businessmen.

The first two books Sartre wrote as an adult were inspired by his reading of Nietzsche and a biography of Nietzsche. The first was a novel entitled *A Defeat* (*Une défaite*) written about 1927-28 and based on the story of Nietzsche's unrequited love for Richard Wagner's wife Cosima. The second, *The Legend of Truth* (*La Légende de la vérité*), was written between 1929 and 1931. It consisted of essays in the form of myths on three different kinds of truth: the certainty of science, the probability of philosophy, and the living truth of the solitary man. Both books were rejected for publication, and Sartre moved on to other interests.

He began to concentrate in earnest on his belief in the irreducibility and contingency of the physical world. He believed that ordinary objects like tables and trees had a reality that is independent of (i.e. not reducible to) our perceptions and ideas of them. He also believed that this reality, the existence of physical objects, is unexplainable. The world exists, but there is no reason for it to exist. It is not, for example, the necessary result of divine creation or, as Hegel thought, the unfolding of spirit through space and time. Furthermore, he believed that the irreducibility and contingency of the physical world could be known through direct experience. What Sartre lacked was a method and language for developing these beliefs.

The break for Sartre came in an unexpected way. During a visit to Paris in 1933, Sartre and Beauvoir spent an evening with their friend Raymond Aron, who was studying phenomenology at the French Institute in Berlin. Beauvoir describes what happened:

We spent an evening together at the Bec de Gaz on the Rue Montparnasse. We ordered the specialty of the house, Apricot Cocktails; Aron said, pointing to his glass: 'You see my dear fellow, if you are a phenomenologist, you can talk about this cocktail and make philosophy out of it!' Sartre turned pale with emotion at this. Here was just the thing that he had been longing to achieve for years—to describe objects just as he saw and touched them, and extract philosophy from the process. . . Sartre decided to make a serious study of [Husserl], and took the necessary steps to succeed Aron at the French Institute in Berlin for the coming year" (Beauvoir 1966, 112).

In September of 1933, Sartre began his studies in Berlin. Adolph Hitler had been appointed Chancellor in January, and the grip of Nazism had begun to tighten on all aspects of life in Germany, as it would a few years later on Europe as a whole. But in 1933 Sartre was less concerned with the future of Europe than with his own development as a philosopher and writer. He spent his mornings reading Husserl and his evenings working on a new novel. He learned that Husserl had been educated as a mathematician, not as a philosopher, and had turned to philosophy in order to gain a better understanding of the foundations of mathematics. Although Husserl's philosophical interests soon expanded beyond mathematical phenomena, he sought to bring to philosophy the methodological rigor of science and mathematics. The result was an ambitious program for a science of appearances. (The word phenomenology means the science of that which appears or shows itself.) By 1911, Husserl thought of phenomenology as a rigorous descriptive science for examining whatever appears, insofar as it appears and only insofar as it appears.

In the fall of 1934, Sartre returned to his teaching duties at Le Havre braced with new optimism about his future. Inspired by Husserl, he adopted key insights and methods from phenomenology and began using them in original ways. His first book to be published, *The Imagination* (*L'Imagination, 1936*), used phenomenological methods to address the longstanding philosophical and psychological problem of how to explain the difference between a perception and an image. Everyone recognizes that seeing a wolf is different from imagining a wolf, but what exactly is that difference? Sartre rejects the view that both are ideas in the mind: the perception being a vivid idea and the image less vivid. For Sartre, nothing is *in* the mind. Imagining and perceiving are both ways of being conscious of the world at large.

11

When I perceive a wolf I am conscious of the wolf as present, when I imagine a wolf I am conscious of the wolf as absent or non-existent. *The Imagination* was followed in 1937 by a book-length essay entitled "The Transcendence of the Ego" ("*La Transcendance de l'ego*" 1937). Here again, Sartre affirms the view that consciousness has nothing inside of itself: it is pure awareness. But if this is so, how can we explain the continuity of consciousness? What is that connects my thoughts now with the thoughts I had ten minutes ago? Why do I recognize those past thoughts as *mine*? To do deal with this problem, Husserl had posited a "transcendental ego": an "I" behind consciousness that connects and constitutes the stream of conscious experiences. Sartre rejects Husserl's solution and argues that the connections between my consciousness now and my consciousness at other times are the connections my consciousness now creates for itself. There is an ego, says Sartre, but that ego is an ideal object, a fiction, that consciousness invents to reinforce its sense of identity. Consciousness itself is:

> [an] impersonal spontaneity. It determines its existence at each instant, without being able to conceive of anything *before* it. Thus each instance of our conscious life reveals to us creation *ex nihilo* [from nothing]. Not a new arrangement but a new existence. (Sartre, *TE* 1957, 98-99)

This bold thesis would become part of the foundation for his most important philosophical work.

Sartre's other major project at this time was his novel on the theme of contingency. It had begun as a poem on the irreducible contingency of a chestnut tree, but Sartre had no gift for poetry and the result was embarrassing. He gave up the poem and began writing a pamphlet which combined phenomenological description with a fictional speaker. He showed it to Beauvoir who found it promising but suggested that he use his talents as a writer and his fondness for mystery novels to work the theme of contingency into a novel with a real story line. He took her advice and began working on a novel entitled *Melancholia* (taking the name from a famous engraving by Albrecht Dürer). The setting for the novel is a fictional seaport city called Bouville [literally Mudville], modeled closely on Le Havre. The main character, Antoine Roquentin, is a thirty-year old intellectual who has come to Bouville to conduct research in the city's archives for a historical biography he is attempting to complete. The novel is written in the form of diary, which Roquentin keeps in an effort to makes sense out of his increasingly oppressive struggles with contingency. He is afflicted, on the one hand, with recurrent bouts of nausea that make him acutely aware of the independent reality of physical objects. He is troubled, on the other hand, by the contingency and meaninglessness of his own life. Roquentin's gradual discoveries about himself and the world constitute a remarkably interesting tale: a kind metaphysical mystery novel. In 1936, Sartre submitted his novel to the distinguished publisher Gallimard. Confident of the magnitude of his achievement, he was shocked when his book was rejected. "I had put the whole of myself into the book . . ." he said, "To reject it was to reject me" (Hayman 1992, 123-124). When he met Beauvoir at Christmastime, he could not hold back his tears. Fortunately, two of his friends arranged for the book to be reconsidered. After reading book himself, Gaston Gallimard met with Sartre. His only objection was the title of the book. He suggested that the book be called *Nausea (La Nausée)*. Sartre agreed, and Gallimard scheduled *Nausea* for release in 1938. There is little doubt that *Nausea* is one of Sartre's most enduring accomplishments. It may well be the most densely philosophical novel ever written.

By 1939, Sartre had achieved his ambition of becoming a writer. Although far from famous and still teaching at a *lycée* (in Neuilly), his essays, short stories, literary criticism, and new novel were being printed and read. In Paris especially, he was gaining recognition as a new voice in French literature. Five of his short stories were published as a collection under the title *The Wall (Le Mur)*. The lead story of the collection, also called "The Wall," dealt with the civil war that was going on Spain and the psychology of men of waiting to be executed. This story may also reflect Sartre's growing interest in Heidegger's revolutionary book *Being and Time*—especially Heidegger's views on authenticity as "freedom towards death." Another story in the collection, "The Childhood of a Leader" (*"L'Enfance d'un chef"*) contains elements of Sartre's theory of bad faith (self-deception) and the formation of personal identity in childhood. In addition, Sartre completed the second half of his study of imagination, *The Psychology of Imagination (L' Imaginaire)* and most of a novel, *The Age of Reason (L'Age de raison)*.

During the same period, Sartre also wrote (in three months!) 400 pages of a treatise on phenomenological psychology which he planned to call "The Psyche" (*"Le Psyché"*). Although only one fragment of this treatise was published, that fragment *The Emotions: Outline of a Theory (Esquisse d'une théorie des émotions)* is a significant work in its own right and part of the foundation for Sartre's later philosophy.

This book registers Sartre's growing debt to Heidegger's *Being and Time*. He borrows from Heidegger the general thesis that emotions are not internal states which sweep over us but ways that we choose to be in the world. He then argues that strong emotions such as fear, joy, anger, and sadness are also ways in which we choose to deceive ourselves about the world. According to Sartre, strong emotions typically involve physiological change to one's body (changes in blood pressure, muscle tension, breathing, etc.), but they always involve attempts to transform the world (beyond one's body) by means of magic. Thus, by permitting myself to slip into the grip of a strong emotion such as anger, I transform the object of my resentment into something inherently hateful, something that stains the world and needs to be eliminated--if not physically at least symbolically. Furthermore, for the object of my emotion the realities that guide practical behavior are "magically" suspended or adjusted. I may, for example, see the object of my anger as far more evil and powerful than any rational assessment could possibly justify.

Given Sartre's remarkable productivity as a philosopher and writer and his obligations as a teacher, one might imagine that he had little time left for anything else. Yet he worked with astonishing speed and somehow found time for vacations with Beauvoir, the pleasures of café life, correspondence with friends, and a number of extended love affairs. Although Beauvoir would have preferred a more monogamous relationship, she yielded to Sartre's preference for complete sexual freedom and, over the years, had affairs with both men and women, including an intense affair with American novelist Nelson Algren. Sartre's relationship with women, other than Beauvoir, tended to follow a curious pattern. Although he enjoyed being intimate with women, sexual intercourse was not his primary source of pleasure:

> I was more a masturbator of women than a copulator. . . . For me what mattered most in a sexual relationship was embracing, caressing, moving my lips over a body . . . I came erect quickly, easily: I made love often, but without very much pleasure. Just a little pleasure at the end, but fairly second-rate (Hayman, 1992, 144).

Sartre liked having affairs with women who, in addition to being young and pretty, were exotic, childish, or mysterious—women whose intuitive personalities contrasted with his own relentlessly analytic frame of mind. Among Sartre's earliest conquests were two sisters, Olga and Wanda Kosakiewicz, the daughters of a Russian nobleman.

Sometimes, Sartre's relationships with women began with seduction and ended with adoption. By the 1960s, Sartre was providing financial support and acting roles for a number of current or former mistresses. In March 1965, he legally adopted his last and youngest mistress, Arlette Elkaïm, a Jewish woman from Algeria.

C. The War Years: 1939-1944

On September 1, 1939, Germany invaded Poland and World War II began. Sartre was called up for duty and sent to a small village thirteen miles from the front to take wind measurements for the French artillery. After smashing Poland, Germany waited for six months before taking action again. But the following spring, the German army swept through Holland and Belgium and into northeastern France with astonishing and overwhelming force. The French military lacked the leadership, technology, and will to deal with the German *Blitzkrieg*, and the army of France collapsed in defeat. One of the soldiers killed during the invasion was Sartre's old friend, Paul Nizan. Sartre was taken prisoner on the morning of his 35th birthday, June 21, 1940. The soldiers who captured him were the first German soldiers he had seen since the war began.

Under the terms of the 1940 armistice, all French prisoners-of-war were required to remain in captivity until the end of the war. Sartre was sent to Stalag XII-D in Trier near the Luxembourg border. Despite the usual hardships of life in a prisoner-of-war camp, he learned to enjoy the rough company of his fellow prisoners. "What I liked at the camp was the feeling of belonging to a crowd." (Hayman 1992, 176) He also became friends with several of the priests in the camp. One priest, Fr. Marius Perrin, was interested in phenomenology and Sartre tutored him by translating Heidegger's *Being and Time* into French. At Christmas, Sartre wrote and staged a "resistance" play, *Bariona*, about a rebel leader who plans to strangle the infant Jesus in order to keep up the spirit of rebellion against the Romans in ancient Judea. In the end, the wise man Balthazar, played by Sartre, convinces Bariona to spares the infant by offering an existentialist gospel: "Christ is here to teach you that you are responsible for yourself and your suffering." (Sartre, *B* 1974, 2:130). Bariona accepts Christ as an ally and leads his men against the Romans in the name of freedom. One member of the audience who misunderstood the point of the play was so touched by Balthazar's speech that he subsequently converted to Christianity. For

Sartre, life in Stalag XII-D had proven rather gratifying, but he had other goals to fulfill. After nine months of captivity, he used a fake medical certificate to obtain his release. Back in Paris, Sartre found himself in an occupied city. Although living under Nazi occupation was humiliating, it was not too difficult at first for French citizens who were neither Jews, Communists, nor recognized political opponents. The Nazis were eager to win support from the French, whom they viewed as a kindred people, and therefore treated them far better than they did the conquered peoples of Eastern Europe. They permitted the southern half of France (the Vichy régime) to govern itself as a closely-watched ally under the leadership of a retired French general, the eighty-five year old Marshal Henri Pétain. They also hoped to lure French intellectuals into collaborating with Nazi leadership.

Sartre had returned to Paris full of plans. After reestablishing contact with his friends and lovers, he put the finishing touches on *The Age of Reason* and produced a new system of philosophy, inspired in part by his reading of Heidegger. (The fact that Sartre was borrowing from Heidegger, a Nazi Party member, may have helped him to avoid harassment by the occupation officials in Paris.) Having laid the foundations of a system through his phenomenological studies of imagination, the ego, and emotions, and his exploration of contingency in *Nausea*, he was ready to complete the final synthesis. He had begun the writing while still a prisoner-of war. Now at liberty, he finished his single most important work: *Being and Nothingness: An Essay in Phenomenological Ontology* (*L'Être et le Néant: Essai d'ontologie phénoménologique*). It was published by Gallimard in June 1943.

Given the magnitude of this book and its centrality to Sartre's career, there is no responsible way to summarize its conclusions in the space of a few paragraphs. I will spend most of the next three chapters on *Being and Nothingness*. For the purposes of this chapter, it will suffice to consider just three theses that are particularly important for understanding Sartre's later work. The theses are: limitless freedom, limitless responsibility, and the futility of bad faith. For readers unfamiliar with the free will debate and Sartre's unusual take on this debate, these theses may sound quite strange at first. The following paragraphs are intended as a starting place, a first exposure. What is said here will be amplified and clarified in Chapter 4.

Limitless Freedom

In *Being and Nothingness*, Sartre defends the remarkable thesis

16

that the being of human beings is freedom. Part of what he means by that is that human beings do not merely *have* free will, they are freedom incarnate. To exist as a human being is to be an embodied agent-consciousness. Through our bodies we are able to be in the world, to be conscious of the world, and to act on the world. But consciousness remains causally independent of the world. It is also causally independent of its past. What has happened in the past, be it physical or mental, cannot causally determine my present choice because I am separated from that past by a gap across which causality cannot travel: I am separated from that past by nothingness (*néant*). Thus, I can truly say of any conscious action I have ever done "I could have done otherwise, even if everything else had been precisely the same." According to Sartre, only freedom itself can limit freedom. This means two things. First, we are not free not to choose. We are, says Sartre, "condemned to be free" (Sartre *BN* 1956, 439). Second, we cannot control the free will of others.

Although my freedom is limitless, it is never abstract. Freedom for Sartre is always freedom *in* a particular situation, and in every situation there are givens (facticity) to which freedom must respond. My body, my past, and my relations with others are among the factors that define my facticity. I may want to fly like a bird, or like Superman, but my body is not capable of flight. In order to fly, I will need to choose and use appropriate technology. I may regret having said angry words to my friend, but I cannot change the past. At most, I can change the *meaning* the past will have in the future. I can do that by apologizing, making amends, promising not to get angry again, etc. I may wish that my boss had a higher opinion of my abilities, but I cannot change his opinion by wishful thinking. If he doubts my abilities for objective reasons, I may be able to change his future opinion by demonstrating abilities that he has not yet recognized. If he doubts my abilities for prejudicial reasons (e.g. because I am woman, a black, a Jew, etc.), then my efforts to demonstrate unrecognized abilities may be futile. He too is free, and he may choose to remain in bad faith.

Limitless Responsibility

Sartre also tries to show that since human beings are free they are responsible, not only for the lives they lead, but also, for the world in which they live. If, for example, I am born into poverty, then my opportunities for achieving a life free of want and grueling labor may be very limited, but it is up to me to decide how to deal with my condition. I may endure it as my "natural" state or I may find it intolerable and strive to escape from it. (Although to choose the latter, I must first conceive a better condition, and, by contrast, recognize the deficiencies of my present condition.) Yet this is only half of the story, for I must also share responsibility for a world, my world, in which people are born into poverty, go to war, etc. The soldier who is called up to fight in a war assumes responsibility, not only for his own condition, but for the war itself. If I fight in the war, rather than desert or commit suicide, I make the war mine. I cannot excuse myself by saying "I did not declare the war" or "I don't agree with its aims." Sartre quotes with favor Jules Romains' remark: "In war there are no innocent victims," and adds for good measure: "We have the war we deserve" (Sartre *BN* 1956, 554-555).

The Futility of Living in Bad Faith

Limitless freedom and limitless responsibility might not be overwhelming burdens if we were not conscious of them. But according to Sartre, we are conscious of them. In fact, we are directly and continuously conscious of them through the emotion of anguish. What prevents us from feeling anguished most of the time are our persistent efforts to hide from freedom and responsibility through self-deception or, what Sartre prefers to call, bad faith (*mauvaise foi*). Through bad faith, we strive to achieve the kind of being that non-conscious things have. We strive to be a writer, or a parent, or a boss in the way that a rock is a rock or a table is a table. (Rocks never have to choose or excuse what they are.)

Furthermore, Sartre links this theory of bad faith to a psychoanalytic theory of human development. He argues that between the ages of eight and twelve, every child makes a fundamental choice of being. The child fastens on to a vaguely formulated project of self-realization (e.g. to be a writer, a leader, a solitary, a failure, a thief) and begins building a life in pursuit of that project. What makes this project more than just an early step in the process of growing up is that it is undertaken in bad faith. It is undertaken as a personal destiny, something one *has to be* rather than something one has freely chosen *to do*. According to Sartre, most people spend their lives in bad faith passionately seeking to complete their projects of being and thereby escape freedom. But this is a futile endeavor. "Man," Sartre declares, "is a useless passion" (Sartre, *BN* 1956, 615).

Although Sartre had always favored liberal socialism over capitalism, fascism, and Soviet-style communism, he had never engaged in any kind of political of action. (He thought it pointless to vote.) When his friend Nizan joined the French Communist Party (PCF) in 1929, he was impressed by his friend's commitment but unwilling to make a political commitment of his own. By 1941 that had changed. His experiences as soldier and prisoner-of-war, especially his production of the Christmas play *Bariona*, had shown him the possibility of acting in solidarity with large numbers of people and the potential of theatre as a vehicle for political communication. Within a month of his return to Paris, Sartre founded a resistance group called "Socialism and Freedom." It was made up of his "family" (Beauvoir, Olga and Wanda and Kosakiewicz, J.-L. Bost, Jean Pouillon,) and friends (like Maurice Merleau-Ponty) and committed to encouraging French men and women to maintain their pride and avoid collaboration with the Germans. During the summer of 1941, Sartre and Beauvoir slipped across the border into the Free Zone (Vichy France) for a bicycle trip and a chance to recruit converts for Socialism and Liberty. They approached two of the most famous writers in France, André Gide and André Malraux, but neither was interested in joining Sartre's group. Britain was fighting for its own life and the Soviet Union was reeling under the invasion that Germany had launched in June of 1941. What, they asked, could French civilians do?

Sartre and Beauvoir returned to Paris disappointed with their efforts and a few months later dissolved Socialism and Freedom. But the French Resistance was really just beginning. By December 1942, the Soviet Union had stopped the German advance at Stalingrad, Britain was no longer under threat of invasion, and British and American troops were rapidly gaining control of North Africa. In France, followers of Charles de Gaulle, the French colonel who had fled to England into 1940 rather than surrender, and French Communists began to build resistance organizations that carried out espionage, sabotage and relayed valuable information to Allied agents. Although Sartre was willing to do what he could for the Resistance, his actual contributions were minor. As a politically independent philosopher, he tended to be seen as unreliable and/or ineffectual. In 1944, his friend Albert Camus provided Sartre with writing assignments for *Combat,* the underground newspaper that Camus was helping to edit.. However, Sartre's most memorable contribution to the cause of resistance was his play *The Flies* (*Les Mouches*).

Like *Bariona*, *The Flies* used an ancient story to carry a message of empowerment and resistance to French men and women without provoking German authorities into closing the play. The story in this case is the Greek legend of the House of Atreus, a tale of family bloodguilt and revenge set around the time of the Trojan War. The elements of the story are these: Agamemnon, King of Argos, sacrifices one of his daughters in order to appease the gods and sail to Troy; when he returns home his wife, Clytemnestra, and her lover, Aegistheus, take revenge by killing Agamemnon; seven years later Agamemnon's son, Orestes, returns from abroad, kills his mother and her lover, and frees his sister, Electra.

A distinctive feature of Sartre's play is the way that guilt has been dispersed among all the citizens of Argos. Instead of assuming full responsibility for their own crime, the new King and Queen have convinced the people of Argos that everyone shares in the guilt and needs to suffer for that guilt. The furies of guilt have turned into flies, and they are everywhere. The guilt of Argos' rulers has become collective guilt, and everybody must suffer for it. Since this was essentially the message that Marshal Pétain had conveyed to the French people, there is a clear parallel between ancient Argos and France during World War II. After Orestes kills his mother and Aegistheus he is approached by the god Jupiter, who is willing to support Orestes as king as long as he agrees to maintain Argos' cult of collective guilt. Orestes refuses, insisting that he alone is responsible and that Jupiter has no power over him. Of course, Jupiter does have some power over him. He has the power to punish him and even to kill him. What Orestes means is that that Jupiter does not control his freedom.

Although *The Flies* was not particularly successful in 1943, either financially or critically, it inspired Sartre to write additional plays. In 1944, Sartre wrote and staged a one act play entitled *No Exit*. It was a philosophical play based on ideas that Sartre had developed in *Being and Nothingness*. It had little to do with the war or the political scene in France, but it was brilliant. *No Exit* has proved to be Sartre's most popular play and is often cited as a model for the Theater of Ideas.

D. Humanistic Existentialist: 1945-1951

In August of 1944, Paris was liberated from German occupation. Allied troops, led by De Gaulle's Free French Forces, entered the city amidst sporadic sniper fire and wildly cheering crowds. Although Hitler had ordered that Paris be destroyed rather than surrendered to the allies, his orders were disobeyed. In October, the Allies recognized De Gaulle as head of the French provisional government. On April 30, 1945, Hitler committed suicide in his bunker in Berlin. Eight days later, Germany surrendered unconditionally, and the war in Europe was over.

It was not until after World War II that Sartre became well known outside of France. The liberation of France meant that his books and plays could be published, circulated, translated, and performed abroad. As Sartre's fame spread, new readers often assumed that the gloomy vision of human existence presented in works like *Nausea, Being and Nothingness* and *No Exit* was a reaction to Hitler's domination of Europe and the horrors of World War II. What, they asked themselves, could explain the bleakness of Sartre's worldview—his emphasis on the bankruptcy of humanism, the meaninglessness of the universe, the absence of God, endless conflict with other people, and the bad faith of our deepest aspirations? The answer seemed obvious: his experiences in a nightmare world in which the veneer of civilization had been stripped away and human beings had been exposed at their weakest and ugliest. Ironically, the opposite was true! Sartre's experiences during World War II made him more optimistic not more pessimistic. His experiences as a soldier, a prisoner-of-war, and a minor player in the French Resistance opened his eyes to the possibility of collective action, personal heroism, and political commitment.

A few days after the liberation of Paris, Sartre wrote:

> We were never more free than under the Nazi Occupation. We had lost all our rights, beginning with our right to speak. We were insulted daily and had to bear those insults in silence. On one pretext or another—as workers, Jews, political prisoners—Frenchmen were deported. . . . Every instant we lived to the full meaning of that banal little phrase "All men are mortal." Everyone of us who knew the truth about the Resistance asked himself anxiously "If they torture me, shall I be able to keep silent?" Thus the basic question of freedom was set before us; and we were brought to the point of the deepest knowledge a man can have of himself. The secret of man is not his Oedipus complex or his inferiority complex; it is the limit of his own freedom; his capacity for standing up to torture and death (Cranston 1966, 10).

The year 1944 was a year of profound transition for Sartre. It was a year in which ideas that had been simmering through the war years replaced some of the older ideas that he had woven into the fabric of his philosophy. Although he did not give up the terminology that he had adopted in *Being and Nothingness*, he began to take his philosophy and life in a new direction. He began to emphasize the possibilities of authenticity and commitment.

21

This change in direction is reflected in his trilogy "The Roads to Liberty." The first two volumes, *The Age of Reason* and *The Reprieve (Le Sursis)* were published in 1945 but written before that; the third volume *Troubled Sleep (La Mort dans l'âme)* was written mainly in 1948 and published in 1949. In this volume, the trilogy's anti-hero, Mathieu, finds freedom and purpose in the heroism of self-sacrifice during the German offensive of 1940. Without hope of success or even survival, he chooses to fight to the death from his perch in a church steeple rather than surrender. His goal is to last for fifteen minutes.

This focus on commitment is also reflected in Sartre's willingness to embrace the label of existentialist and to defend existentialism as a humanistic philosophy of commitment. Without a doubt, Sartre's best known essay is the printed version of a lecture that he gave at the Club Maintenant on October 28, 1945, entitled "Existentialism is a Humanism" (*"L'Existentialisme est un humanisme"*). One purpose of this essay was to define existentialism and to distinguish atheistic from religious existentialism. A second purpose was to show that existentialism was not a philosophy of despair, solitude, and hopelessness, but a kind of humanism. A third purpose was to demonstrate that existentialism offered a viable alternative to Christianity and Marxism, not only as a way of understanding the human condition but also as a basis for choice and action. To make good on this claim, Sartre had to show that his brand of existentialism had ethical implications about what people ought or ought not to do. Near the end of the essay, he outlines some strategies for deriving ethical conclusions from his existentialist premises. Still, the question remained: could this outline become a coherent theory?

Actually, Sartre had already promised to develop the ethical implications of his philosophy. In *Being and Nothingness*, he had promised a "future work" that would examine the possibility of choosing freedom as a value rather being, authenticity rather than bad faith. (Sartre *BN* 1956, 70n., 627-628). But his critics doubted that he could fulfill this promise. Any systematic account of the human condition is bound to offer insights into why people do what they do, and such insights may be useful for understanding areas of human conduct that are ethically important. Thus, a philosophy like Sartre's is bound to offer insights for *descriptive ethics*. If, however, one is looking for guidance on what people *ought* to do, on *norms* (i.e. standards) of good or bad, right or wrong, then something more is required. In order demonstrate that a particular account of the human condition can support *normative ethics*, it is necessary to find a normative anchor within that account. (Remember that 'normative' does not mean 'normal.') In Judaism, Christianity, and Islam that anchor is a single, perfect divinity. In some versions of Marxism that anchor is the inescapable progression of history. For some philosophers that anchor is a theory of human nature, for example: that man is a rational animal (Aristotle); that man is a pleasure-seeker (Bentham and Mill), that man is a power-seeker (Nietzsche). The trouble with Sartre's account of the human condition is that it seemed to offer no place to anchor a normative ethics. He denied the existence of God, he denied that there was an inescapable progression in history, and he denied that human beings had a fixed nature. What he attributed to humans were nasty dispositions to deceive themselves, deny their contingency, and engage in conflict with one another.

From 1945 until 1951, Sartre and Beauvoir devoted considerable time and talent to the quest for a normative theory of existentialist ethics. But the results of their efforts were ultimately disappointing. On the one hand, they had impressive success in applying Sartre's theory of bad faith and Beauvoir's theory of the socially constructed Other to the analysis of anti-Semitism, gender discrimination, and color-based prejudice. Sartre's *Anti-Semite and Jew* (*Réflexions sur la question juivre* 1946) and Beauvoir's *The Second Sex* (*Le Deuxieme Sexe* 1949) are brilliant examples of philosophical psychology and sociology in areas of ethical importance. Both books are excellent on the prejudices they treat, although Beauvoir's account of what it means to be a woman is far superior to Sartre's narrow account of what it means to be a Jew. Sartre also framed some promising insights on the issues of "blackness" and color-prejudice in a preface to an anthology of African poetry entitled *Black Orpheus* (*Orphée Noir* 1948.) Impressive, too, are Sartre's discussions of "committed literature": his efforts to demonstrate that writers of prose ought to consider writing a form of action and write on behalf of social and political causes. *What is Literature* (*Qu'est-ce que la littérature?* 1947) remains an insightful exploration of the intersection between ethics and aesthetics.

On the other hand, neither Sartre nor Beauvoir had much success in creating a coherent ethical theory. Beauvoir's *The Ethics of Ambiguity* (*Pour une morale de l'ambiguïté* 1947) amplified the outline Sartre had drawn in "Existentialism is a Humanism" by providing a richer array of examples and by responding to critics of existentialist ethics, but it did not supply the missing theoretical framework. In 1947-48, Sartre began compiling extensive notes for a book on ethics. He called these notes "Notebooks for an Ethics, Volume I and Volume II," but he did not weave them into a completed text or attempt to publish them. Indeed, he insisted that they not be published until after his death (Sartre, *NFE* 1992, xxiii). He did, however, incorporate some of his reflections on ethics into his play *The Devil and the Good God* (*Le Diable et le bon dieu* 1951) and his long psycho-biography of Jean Genet, *Saint Genet: Actor and Martyr* (*Saint Genet; comédian et martyr* 1952).

Although Sartre and Beauvoir had reached an impasse in the development of a normative theory of existentialist ethics, they had no hesitation about committing themselves and their work to political and social causes. As writers with rapidly growing international reputations and the chief exponents of existentialism, they now had the capacity to reach large audiences. They also had sufficient income to resign from their teaching posts and use that time for other purposes. Too famous to work comfortably in cafes, they found new living quarters and wrote at home. (After the death Joseph Mancy in 1946, Sartre's mother bought an apartment on the Rue Bonaparte in Paris and Sartre moved in with her. He remained there for sixteen years.)

Fame also brought them invitations to visit and lecture abroad. In 1945, Sartre spent four months in the United States. During his stay in New York, he fell in love with Dolores Vanetti, who had once been an actress in Paris. For a brief time this relationship was so intense that Sartre seriously considered taking a two-year teaching position at Columbia University. But Sartre did not like or understand the United States. Unable to speak English, antagonistic to capitalism, and rightfully indignant at American traditions of racial discrimination, he felt little kinship with the United States.

The fame that Sartre and Beauvoir had achieved guaranteed that their opinions would be noticed, but political effectiveness required a way of responding quickly to current events. To provide themselves with a fast and dependable outlet for their writing, they had joined in September of 1944 with a group of friends (including Maurice Merleau-Ponty and Raymond Aron) to produce a new monthly journal. The name of this journal, *Les Temps Modernes* (Modern Times), was chosen in part because of Sartre's fondness for a 1936 Charlie Chaplin movie by that title and in part because the journal was committed to dealing with contemporary issues. Although *Les Temps Modernes* was pitched to a highly literate audience rather than to the working class, whose interests they hoped to serve, it enabled Sartre and Beauvoir to carry on a monthly dialogue with other intellectual and ideological leaders.

Yet political commitment turned out to be nastier and more complicated than they had expected. In America, the start of the Cold

War led to anti-Communist crusades and made it difficult to defend any political program that was left of center, even the mildest forms of socialism. In France, the start of the Cold War led to bitter divisions across a much broader spectrum of political ideologies. For example, the elections of 1951 left the French Assembly with most of its seats split fairly evenly among six political parties, the largest being the Gaullists (RPF), the Socialists (SFIO), and the Communists (PCF). Until 1952, Sartre and Beauvoir attempted to steer an independent course. They rejected both American-style capitalism and Soviet-style Communism. Fearing American domination of Europe, they opposed NATO. (Although they agreed with the U.S. on the creation of Israel.) They condemned the Gaullists and other centrists for their attachment to American capitalism and support for French colonialism. (The French had been fighting in Vietnam since 1946). They praised the Soviet Union for striving to perfect socialism, but they criticized its repression of civil liberties, brutal labor camps, and imperialistic stance toward other communist nations. They attacked the French Communist Party (PCF) for slavish obedience to the Soviet party line and unwillingness to tolerate independent thinking in its own ranks. They admired Marxist ideology for its staunch commitment to the interests of the working class, but disagreed with its insistence that human action and history were causally determined. These views were advanced by Sartre not only in essays but also in his novel, *Troubled Sleep*, his play, *Dirty Hands (Les Mains Sales*, 1948), and his film script, *In the Mesh* (*L'Engrenage*, 1948). For a period of eighteen months, Sartre served on the management committee of a new political party, The Revolutionary Peoples Assembly (RDP), but he broke with the leaders of the party when they favored France's involvement in NATO.

E. Communist Fellow Traveler: 1952-1956

In 1952, Sartre changed his political stance and began a four-year period as a supporter of the French Communist Party, the *Parti Communist Français*, or PCF. Although he never became a member of the PCF, he was a fellow traveler and sought to defend the party against its critics. The reasons for this change were both philosophical and practical. One philosophical reason was his failure to develop a normative theory for existentialist ethics. This failure had made him reconsider the advantages of anchoring ethical commitment in a Marxist interpretation of history. Another philosophical reason was his growing suspicion that *Being and Nothingness* had exaggerated the real independence of individual human beings. On a political plane, Sartre had become convinced that the only party capable of uniting the workers of France and bringing about revolutionary change in the social order was the PCF, therefore anti-Communism in all its forms hurt the long-term interest of the working class. He had begun to accept the Communist argument that one should avoid public criticism of the PCF or the Soviet Union, even when such criticism was valid, because it harmed the working class and helped the enemies of the working class.

Yet Sartre's conversion in 1952 also owed a good deal to the events of the moment. One events was the arrest of Jacques Duclos, leader of the Communists in the National Assembly. In retaliation for a public demonstration that had ended in violence, several leading Communists, including Duclos, were arrested in May 1952. Two pigeons were found in Duclos' car, and he was charged with espionage on the assumption that they were carrier pigeons. In fact, he was planning to eat the pigeons. (Pigeons are considered a delicacy in France.) The Communists tried to organize a protest strike for June 2, but the strike failed and the right-wing press celebrated this failure as a sign that the Communists were losing credibility with workers.

In June 1952 Sartre exploded in anger. He had finally come to see for himself "how much shit can be crammed into a middle-class heart" (Sartre, *SBH*, 1978, 72). Writing about this moment years later, he said:

> My vision was transformed: an anti-Communist is a swine, I can see no way out of that, and I never will. . . . After ten years of brooding about it, I had reached a breaking point and I needed only a gentle push. In the language of the Church, this was a conversion (Hayman 1987, 301-302).

Sartre's conversion to active support for PCF at home and the Communist cause abroad led to profound changes in his life. His defense of Communism and his condemnation of anti-Communism in *The Communists and Peace* (*Les Communistes et la Paix*, 1952, 1954) provoked public quarrels with Albert Camus and Maurice Merleau-Ponty. After a bitter exchange of letters in the *Les Temps Modernes*, Sartre never saw Camus again. Merleau-Ponty, who had initially been responsible for pushing Sartre toward a more sympathetic view of the Communists, resigned as Editor-in-Chief of *Les Temps Modernes*. Sartre had broken with Raymond Aron in 1947, but their differences now became wider and angrier. Aron, for example, characterized as "hyper-Stalinism" Sartre's 1953 essay accusing the United States of fascism for executing Julius and Ethel Rosenberg as atomic spies. In May 1954, Sartre visited the Soviet Union. Stalin had died the year before and Nikita Khrushchev was now first secretary of the Central Committee. A year and a half later, Khurshchev would startle both Communists and anti-Communists around the world by denouncing Stalin's "bloody crimes" proclaiming "de-Stalinization," and conceding that "different roads to Socialism" were possible. Yet Sartre's reports on the USSR in 1954, before de-Stalinization, were overwhelmingly positive. In December, Sartre accepted the post of Vice President of the French-Soviet Association. He also attempted to suppress production of his own play *Dirty Hands* to avoid giving comfort to anti-Communists. The following year, Sartre and Beauvoir spent two months in China as guests of the new Communist regime. But Sartre's stint as a fellow traveler was about to end.

F. Independent Marxist: 1956-1960

In October 1956, the Soviet Union sent an army bristling with tanks and artillery into Hungary to crush an uprising of students, workers, and soldiers who were demanding better standards of living, greater democracy, and more national independence. Khrushchev might have avoided bloodshed by restoring to power Hungary's former liberal premier, Imre Nagy, just he had restored Wladyslaw Gomulka in Poland. Instead, he chose to meet the Hungarians with the might of the Red Army. In the end, between 25,000 and 50,000 Hungarians were killed and thousands more imprisoned. The new premier János Kádár repealed reforms and even abolished his country's "Workers Councils."
Sartre's response was swift and furious. He condemned the Soviet invasion as a crime committed by hypocrites who were trying to outdo Stalinism at the same time they were denouncing it. He blamed the crisis on the Soviet Union's stupid and oppressive policy of trying to impose the same economic structure on all Communist nations. He denounced their use of force as a cruel blunder which presented the Red Army as the enemy of the Hungarian people. In a series of essays under the title "The Ghost of Stalin" (*"Le Fantôme de Stalin*), he argued that the Soviet Union's crime against Hungary was not an accident, but a logical expression of its misguided efforts to interpret

and apply the lessons of Marxism. He was equally scathing in his denunciation of the leaders of the French Communist Party (PCF) for their support of the Soviet Union's crime. "All their comments, all their actions," Sartre said, "are the result of thirty years of lying and sclerosis." (Hayman 1987, 326). He declared that he would never again tie himself to the leaders of the PCF. He resigned from the French-Soviet Association.

Once more, Sartre had readjusted his deepest political convictions in response to current events. This time, however, his new convictions would set him on a course that would continue until almost the end of his life. Although disillusioned with Soviet-style Communism and the PCF, he was more enthusiastic than ever about Marxism. The problem, as he now saw it, was that Communism had twisted and falsified Marxism. His new goal would be to stimulate the reform of Communism by helping to reinterpret Marxism. His new role would be that of an independent Marxist.

For nearly five years, Sartre had not written much except political essays. (He wrote one mediocre play, *Nekrassov,* and began his book on Flaubert.) Now, he was eager to return to technical philosophy and begin a dialogue with Marx and his followers. He was also intent on continuing his longstanding interest in psychobiography, but with a new twist: he would write Marxist biographies.

For most writers, philosophy and biography would be an odd pair of interests, yet for Sartre this pair made sense. Sartre had always aimed his philosophy at trying to explain why people have certain values and do certain things. At the end of *Being and Nothingness,* he sketched an outline of existential psychoanalysis which would allow him to use this framework as a practical tool for analyzing in minute detail the values and actions of individual lives. It resembled Sigmund Freud's theory of psychoanalysis in its emphasis on the influence of childhood experiences on adult behavior, but unlike Freud's theory, it did not appeal to an "unconscious." (In 1959, Sartre wrote a long screenplay about Freud's early career for director John Huston; part of that screenplay was used in Huston's 1962 film, *Freud.*)

With mixed success, Sartre attempted to use his psychoanalytic theory to explain the development of several French writers. He used it in his 1946 biography of the 19th century poet Charles Baudelaire, his unpublished 1948 book on the 19th century poet Stéphane Mallarmé, and his 1952 biography of his friend, the playwright and former thief Jean Genet. Now, as an independent Marxist, Sartre wanted to reconstruct his explanatory framework and psychoanalytic applications based on a Marxist understanding of history. In fact, it was precisely this focus on using Marxist principles to explain the particulars of human history, individual *and* collective, that he intended to be his distinctive contribution to Marxist thought. Phenomenology had enabled him to philosophize about apricot cocktails; Marxism, he believed, would enable him to discover the historical meaning in particular human actions.

For three years, Sartre worked furiously on his new philosophical treatise, *The Critique of Dialectical Reason*. The first fruit of this effort was a remarkable essay on Marxism and existentialism entitled *Search for a Method* (*Questions de méthode*). In this essay Sartre declares that existentialism is not a philosophy on a par with Marxism, but an ideology that needs to be integrated into Marxism. Marxism, he says, is not one philosophy among many, but the *only* legitimate "system of coordinates" for contemporary thought. He claims that attempts to go beyond Marxism today must result in outmoded, pre-Marxist thought. A philosophy of freedom may be possible in the future, but it will not be possible to formulate until there is freedom from need and class oppression for everyone. On the other hand, existentialism must retain its independence as an ideology of human existence until Marxism learns how to incorporate "the human dimension" into its knowledge of history and society (Sartre, *SM* 1963, 181). The perspective of existentialism is necessary because Marxist thinkers have oversimplified Marxism and imposed a mechanistic view on the workings of history.

When *The Critique of Dialectical Reason*, (*La Critique de raison dialectique*, 1960) was published three years later, it included this essay as an introduction. The book as a whole had 755 pages of very fine print. It was longer than *Being and Nothingness* and more difficult to read. Even professional philosophers found it difficult to wade through the thick terminology and multi-page paragraphs that filled this volume. Some pages were clear and powerful, others were obscure and rambling. To help quicken the pace of his writing, Sartre had taken heavy doses of a stimulant called Corydrane. Much that he wrote was not properly edited. He started to write a second volume, but never completed it. Yet, despite its shortcomings, *The Critique of Dialectical Reason* is a work of depth and importance. It does not claim to present a new system of philosophy, but rather to show how the principles established in the 19th century by Karl Marx *ought* to be used to understand the workings of history

What remains unchanged in Sartre's *Critique* is his view of human beings as conscious and purposive agents. On this point, he makes no concessions to Marxists who want to view humans as objects rather than subjects. However, he is willing to concede that the scope of free will and responsibility is a good deal narrower than he previously claimed. He acknowledges that social, economic, and historical factors play a much larger role in influencing and limiting individual choices than he had previously recognized. As he expressed it some years later:

> For I believe that man can always make something out of what is made of him. This is the limit I would accord to freedom: the small movement which makes of a totally conditioned social being someone who does not render back completely what his conditioning has given him. (Sartre, *BEM* 1974, 35).

Some of the ideas in *The Critique of Dialectical Reason* are also presented in a play that Sartre wrote at about the same time, *The Condemned of Altona* (*Les Séquestrés d'Altona*, 1959). This play tells the story of a wealthy German family, who despite their efforts to act decisively and according to their own lights, are thwarted by their own bad faith and by their thorough entanglement in the net of history—family history, German history, and economic class history. In the last act of the play, we learn that during World War II, the play's main character, Franz von Gerlach, tortured to death several Russian peasants. His excuse for this atrocity was the need to extract information about Russian partisans in order to help his men survive during their desperate retreat through Russia, but his primary motive was to preserve his own authority. Although Franz had resisted the efforts of his father to make him a leader and the efforts of Hitler's regime to make him a Nazi, he ended up committing a heartless atrocity in order not to compromise his status as a leader. Sartre also intended Franz's story to suggest a perspective on the atrocities of French officials in Algeria. Indeed, the name Franz (Frantz in the French text) suggests France itself. Over the next eleven years, the course of events, first in the French colony of Algeria, and then in the former French colony of Vietnam would deeply affect Sartre's life.

G. Anti-Imperialist: 1960-1967

At the end of World War II, France had regained its overseas empire, but the age of European imperialism was rapidly coming to an end. In Asia, Africa, and the Middle East, people began demanding independence with demonstrations, strikes, and, sometimes, open warfare. Very quickly, colonies became financial burdens rather than financial assets. The capacity and willingness of the French to hold on to their colonies varied from place to place. In spite of American arms and money, the French military was not able to defeat the Communist-led Viet Minh. After a decisive Viet Minh victory at the battle of Dien Bien Phu in 1954, peace accords were signed in Geneva and the countries of Indochina became independent. The largest of these countries, Vietnam, was temporarily partitioned, with a Communist government in the North and non-Communist government in the South.

The loss of Indochina was a blow to the dignity of France and its hopes of remaining an empire, but that loss was more easily digested than the threat of losing Algeria. Technically, Algeria was part of France, and for many French "settlers," it was home. In 1956, over a million Europeans (mainly of French descent) lived in Algeria. Many belonged to families that had lived there for generations. (Albert Camus, for example, was born and raised in Algeria.) On the other hand, the native population numbered about 8.5 million, mostly poor, illiterate, and subject to constant discrimination. In October 1954, a revolutionary organization, the National Liberation Front (*Front de Libération Nationale*) or FLN, began attacks on French Algerians. In 1955, the French retaliated against FLN massacres with indiscriminate bloodshed based on a policy of "collective responsibility." During the battle of Algiers, the French used torture to intimidate prisoners and extract information.

In 1958, French settlers seized control of Algeria and brought about the fall of the Fourth Republic. Charles de Gaulle returned to power in France and a new constitution for France was approved by referendum, but even de Gaulle's prestige could not bring peace to Algeria. The FLN would not agree to anything less than full independence and the French settlers were determined to resist. In April 1960, four generals in the French army attempted to lead a military coup. When the coup failed, they set up an underground organization, the Secret Army Organization (*Organisation de l'Armée Secrète*) or OAS to commit acts of terror in Algeria and France in hope of preventing a cease-fire in Algeria.

In August 1960, Sartre and Beauvoir were among the first of 121 dissidents who signed a manifesto pledging civil disobedience on behalf of Algerian independence. A month later, Sartre allowed a letter to be written in his name for the trial of his friend Francis Jeanson. The letter, which Sartre had not seen, endorsed Jeanson's aid to Algerian militants, declared that Sartre would have assisted him if asked to do so, and challenged the authority of the government to judge Jeanson.

On October 3, over 6,000 war veterans marched through Paris shouting "French Algeria" and "Shoot Sartre." When Sartre and Beauvoir returned from visits to Cuba and Brazil, they expected to be arrested, like others signers of the manifesto. To their surprise, the police refused to arrest them. De Gaulle had given orders that Sartre and his "family" were to be left alone, saying that one does not arrest Voltaire. The greater danger, however, was from the OAS and other right-wing militants who threatened Sartre with death. In January 1962, a bomb destroyed the apartment where Sartre and his mother had lived for nearly sixteen years. Luckily, Sartre had already moved his mother into a hotel and was sharing a new apartment with Beauvoir.

Although the threats to Sartre's life ended in July 1962, when Algeria became an independent nation, Sartre's involvement with the Algerian crisis helped him to look beyond Europe, the Soviet Union and the United States. Distrustful of Soviet-style Communism and antagonistic to American-style capitalism, he began to invest his hopes in the development of third-world socialism. Both he and Beauvoir had been deeply impressed by their first visit to Castro's Cuba in 1960. Here, perhaps, was a model for a Marxist society in which a visionary leadership worked directly with the masses, avoiding the pitfalls of elitism, oppression, and leaden bureaucracy. Sartre and Beauvoir were also deeply impressed by their meetings with Frantz Fanon, a black physician from Martinique who had been influenced by Sartre's writings, and was now a forceful spokesman for third world liberation. In 1961, Sartre wrote the preface for Fanon's last and most important work, *The Wretched of the Earth* (1961). In that preface, he celebrates the emergence of an independent voice and vision for people of the third world and warns Europeans that the violence they have used to maintain colonial power is about to be repaid in kind. This book was translated in seventeen languages and sold over a million copies.

In 1963, Sartre completed *The Words* (*Les Mots*, 1964), his autobiography to age ten. It was a beautifully written and very personal book, not always accurate on details, but consistently witty and engaging. The principal purpose of *The Words* is to give a psychoanalytic account of how Sartre chose to become a writer and transformed that choice through bad faith into the illusion of a destiny and personal justification. What is odd about the book is that it does so in terms of his earlier existential theory of psychoanalysis and with no explicit attention to Marxist principles of history. *The Words'* most interesting revelation is Sartre's confession that long after he had formulated his views on the futility of living in bad faith, he himself continued to live the lie that he condemned in others.

Fake to the marrow of my bones and hoodwinked, I joyfully wrote about our unhappy state. Dogmatic though I was, I doubted everything except that I was the elect of doubt. I built with one hand what I destroyed with the other, and I regarded anxiety as the guarantee of my security; I was happy. . . . For a long time, I took my pen for a sword ; I now know we're powerless. . . . Culture doesn't save anything or anyone, it doesn't justify (Sartre *Words* 1964, 254-255).

Partially on the strength of this book and its popularity, Sartre was selected to receive the 1964 Nobel Prize for Literature. When he learned that he was likely to be the recipient, he warned the Swedish Academy that he did not want the prize. When they chose him anyway, he refused to accept it and the 26 million francs that went with it. He refused the prize because he did not want to be bought off or even appear to be bought off by the middle-class establishment. He also noted that the Swedish Academy had never before offered this prize to a Marxist writer and the only Soviet writer to receive the prize was the dissident Boris Pasternak.

In the Fall of 1966, Sartre and Beauvoir agreed to serve on the International War Crimes Tribunal that had been initiated by the distinguished British philosopher Lord Bertrand Russell to protest America's escalation of the war in Vietnam and the lethal consequences of that escalation for the civilian population. Although Russell's tribunal had no legal status, it was intended to serve as a public relations platform for shaping world opinion. It was modeled on the Nuremberg trials that the Allies had used after World War II to prosecute Nazi war criminals. The tribunal met in Stockholm and Copenhagen during 1967, and, after months of debate, found the United States guilty of genocidal intent. Sartre, who had been elected Executive President, wrote the final verdict.

In retrospect, Sartre's verdict seems at once perceptive and naïve, cogent and exaggerated. He recognizes that the North Vietnamese, the Viet Cong, and their numerous supporters are committed to total war and will not be stopped by anything short of total defeat. Thus, he reasons that the United States is faced with a choice of making peace [on North Vietnamese terms] or physically eliminating its enemy. Since America is not willing to make peace, it is "guilty of continuing and intensifying the war despite the fact that everyday its leaders realize more accurately . . . that the only way to win is "to free Vietnam of all the Vietnamese" (Sartre, OG 1968, 42). He also draws the clearly erroneous conclusion that the Vietnam War meets all of Hitler's specifications. "Hitler killed Jews because they were Jews. The armed forces of the United States torture and kill men, women, and children in Vietnam *merely because they are Vietnamese*" (Sartre, OG 1968, 42). As enemies of colonialism and champions of people who had suffered under the heel of European powers, Sartre and Beauvoir were unequivocal in their enthusiasm for emerging nations and their sympathy with victims of oppression, like blacks in South Africa. But conflicts *between* victims of oppression posed a different kind of problem. Shortly, before the 1967 Arab-Israeli War, Sartre and Beauvoir visited Egypt and Israel. In both countries they told their hosts that they supported the right of Israel to exist as an independent state and the right of Palestinians living outside of Israel to return home. In both countries they were told these rights were incompatible. As President Nasser of Egypt explained "if Israel took in 1.2 million Palestinians it would no longer be Israel; 'it would burst apart'" (Thompson 1984, 157).

H. Leftist Guardian and Flaubert Biographer: 1968-1972

By 1965 Sartre had given up writing fiction and systematic philosophy, although he continued to write literary criticism and philosophically informed essays. His last major work was a three-volume biography of the 19th century novelist Gustave Flaubert, entitled *The Family Idiot* (*L'Idiot de la famille*, 1971). Many of his working hours from 1968 until his health began to fail in 1972 were spent as a leftist activist (*gauchiste*) on behalf of radical student groups and their newspapers, making public statements on political issues, and giving interviews. As Sartre grew older he sought out the company of young people. In 1965, he adopted his twenty-six year old mistress, Arlette Elkaïm and made her executor of his literary estate. (Although Beauvoir was deeply wounded by Sartre's action at the time, she would eventually follow his example and adopt a young woman, Sylvie le Bon, as her daughter and literary executor.) But Sartre's attraction to young people was philosophical as well as personal and sexual. In *Search for a Method* he had complained about the inability of Marxists of his own generation to think "dialectically" because of their pre-Marxist education. But he held out hope for the future. "Far from being exhausted, Marxism is still very young, almost in its infancy, it has scarcely begun to develop" (Sartre, *SM* 1967, 30).

Two events in 1968 pushed Sartre even further in pinning his hopes on the next generation. One was the invasion of Czechoslovakia by Soviet and other Warsaw Pact troops in August of 1968 in order to crush the liberal Communist government that had come to power earlier in the year. Sartre not only denounced the Soviet Union but also finally severed all ties with its government. He also rebuked Fidel Castro for his support of the invasion. The other event was the outbreak of violent demonstrations by French university students which began in March 1968 and continued for months. The immediate causes of the student uprising were rather concrete: dissatisfaction with overcrowding, too few professors, antiquated educational requirements, and lack of job opportunities after graduation. But these concrete complaints were merged with idealistic concerns about American and Soviet imperialism and the lack of social justice in France.

After violent clashes between police and students in May, Sartre told Radio Luxembourg:

> These youngsters don't want the future of their fathers—our future—a future which proved we were cowardly, weary, worn out, stupefied by total obedience. . . . The only relationship they can have with this university is to smash it (Hayman 1987, 424).

He also arranged an interview with the student's radical young spokesman, Daniel Cohn-Bendit. According to Cohn-Bendit, some of the students in the rebellion had read Marx, "perhaps Bakunin and of the moderns, Althusser, Mao, Guevera, Lefebvre. Nearly, all the militants have read Sartre" (Hayman 1987, 423). The bond was irresistible. Sartre became the grown-up the students could trust, and he, in turn, repaid their trust by employing his fame as a shield to help protect them from violent police and angry officials.

In 1970, Sartre and Beauvoir permitted their names to be listed as "editors" of a Maoist, student newspaper dedicated to the promotion of subversive activities, *La Cause du Peuple*. (Maoism was a version of Communism based on the teaching of China's leader, Mao Zedong. What Sartre did not know was that Mao's atrocities would rival Stalin's.) Among the real editors of this newspaper was a mysterious young man who called himself "Pierre Victor," but whose real name was Benny Lévy. Lévy would play an important role in the last seven years of Sartre's life. For the present, however, he was just one of the student leaders with whom Sartre had joined hands to bring about revolution. For the first time since the Nazi Occupation, Sartre could enjoy being a man of action while experiencing the empowerment that came from being a member of a group united by a common purpose. He appeared at protest rallies, distributed newspapers on the street, and made speeches at factories.

As the French authorities cracked down on the revolutionary left and their publications, Sartre began to experience some embarrassment at his inability to get arrested. In September 1970, he announced that he was making himself available to any revolutionary newspaper in order to force the bourgeoisie (middle-class establishment) to put him on trial or, by failing to put him on trial, to reveal the illegality of its repression. Soon he was listed as "editor" on a dozen extremist newspapers and his name was added to articles he had never seen. One right-wing newspaper, *Minute*, called him "the nation's red cancer" and said he should be in prison (Hayman 187, 445). Finally, in June 1971, he was formally charged with libel of the police and the police system. The charge was based on two unsigned articles in *La Cause du Peuple* and a third unsigned article in a similar publication. On September 24, he appeared in court before two judges, who released him immediately.

Sartre's last major work was his three-volume biography of Flaubert. The first two volumes, *The Family Idiot: Gustave Flaubert from 1821 to 1857* (*L'Idiot de la famille: Gustave Flaubert de 1821 à 1857*) were published in 1971. Although each volume was over a thousand pages long, the two volumes together covered little more than half of Flaubert's life! The third volume, a mere 667 pages, dealt with Flaubert's life and work in relationship to his times.

Why did Sartre choose to write about this mid-19th century novelist whose obsession with the craft of writing prose was so different from Sartre's free-flowing style of composition. Why did he devote so many words to the development of an author whose "art for art's sake" ethic contrasted so sharply with his own dedication to politically committed literature? In the Preface to *The Family Idiot*, he mentions four reasons. The first was personal. Sartre disliked Flaubert and what he stood for. He felt he "had a score to settle" with him. But as he studied Flaubert's letters his dislike changed to empathy and understanding. Second, since Flaubert's life was "objectified" in his work, he offered an exceptional opportunity to examine the relationship between man and work. Third, Flaubert's early fiction and extensive correspondence provided a wealth of personal information: "We might imagine we were hearing a neurotic 'free associating' on the psychoanalyst's couch" (Sartre, *FI* 1981, x). Fourth, "Flaubert, creator, of the 'modern' novel, stands at the crossroads of all our literary problems today" (Sartre, *FI* 1981, x). A fifth reason, which Sartre does not mention in the Preface, but is clearly important, is that Flaubert's life (1821-1880) coincided almost exactly with Karl Marx's life (1818-1883). The historical period that shaped Marx as a philosopher also shaped Flaubert as a writer.

In the first two volumes of *The Family Idiot*, Sartre attempts to explain how Gustave Flaubert became a writer of a very particular kind as a result of the family and social circumstances in which he was raised and the choices he made in response to those circumstances. He speculates about his mother's disappointment with young Gustave for not being the daughter she wanted and his father's disappointment with him for Gustave's slowness in learning to read. He imagines, Flaubert's father, who was a successful doctor with high ambitions for his family, telling his seven-year old son that he will be "the idiot of the family." Thus, at an early age the boy was deprived of a sense of self-worth. Wounded by the judgments of both parents, he saw himself in bleakly negative terms—as a nothingness. What choice did he make in response to these circumstances? According to Sartre, he chose to take revenge on society by reducing everyone to his own negative condition. Of course, he could not do this in reality, but he could do it through the creation of an imaginary world, a world of fiction. Thus, Flaubert gradually formed the project of using the beauty of language to seduce readers into seeing the world as "horrible, cruel, and naked" (Collins 1980, 122).

The third volume of *The Family Idiot* deals with the correspondences between Flaubert's literary works and the history of the bourgeoisie (middle-class establishment) during his most productive years. Although the old aristocracy had been stripped of its hereditary power by the French Revolution (1789-1799), it was not until the industrialization of the 1830s and 1840s that the bourgeoisie came into its own as an immensely wealthy, powerful, and self-conscious class. The distinctive values of this class included: ambition, self-enrichment, hard work, and competition. But the bourgeoisie soon discovered their success was built in part on the misery of the working class. In order to drive up profits, they drove down wages and sacrificed humane working conditions to productivity. Food was scare, infant mortality was rampant, and children were often sent to work before the age of eight. (The bitter poverty of that time is described vividly by Victor Hugo in *Les Miserable*.)

According to Sartre, Flaubert found an enthusiastic audience in the bourgeoisie of his age precisely because this self-conscious class was *comforted* by his grim picture of the world. What Flaubert's novels and stories implied to them was that they were not to blame for the harshness, inequalities, and selfishness in the world. Thus, Flaubert's revenge on his own class became the source of his popularity, and he, in turn, reveled in the heartlessness with which the bourgeoisie confirmed his nasty depiction of them. He was pleased when the failed revolution of 1848 led to the crowning of Napoleon's scheming nephew, Louis Bonaparte, as Emperor Napoleon III. It was a triumph of baseness over idealism.

I. Prophet of Hope and Fraternity: 1973-1980

Following a stroke in 1973, Sartre's health began to deteriorate rapidly. For many years he had treated his body as one might treat an old car, driving it recklessly with little care for its basic needs. He smoked two packs of cigarettes a day, drank a good deal of alcohol, and used sedatives and stimulants to regulate his sleep and work habits. Now, his circulation was so poor that his brains and legs were seriously affected. He had lost control of his bladder. He had diabetes and was going blind. Although he had earned a good deal of money from his writings, he had given nearly all of it way. Fortunately for Sartre, Beauvoir and her sister Hélène, Arlette Elkaïm-Sartre, and his long-time mistresses Wanda Kosakiewicz and Michelle Vian provided him with company and physical care. Nevertheless, by the fall of 1973 Sartre's vision was so bad that he could no longer read or write.

A friend suggested that he hire his former "co-editor" from *La Cause du Peuple*, Benny Lévy to read to him and help him with his writing. Lévy was a Egyptian Jew who had immigrated to France with his family during the Suez crisis of 1956. Although he could not return to Egypt, he had neither French citizenship nor permanent resident status. Employment as Sartre's secretary would help protect him from deportation. (Later, at Sartre's request, the President of France, Valéry Giscard d'Estaing, granted Lévy full citizenship.)

Over the next seven years Sartre and Lévy developed a relationship that astonished and upset most of Sartre's friends. Lévy was a philosophy student with a prodigious memory, a brash personality, and a very good knowledge of Sartre's works. Instead of merely reading to him, Lévy insisted on challenging Sartre by asking him tough questions and engaging him in vigorous debate. Eager for intellectual stimulation, Sartre welcomed Lévy's persistent questioning and presumptuous familiarity. Gradually, Sartre and Lévy formed plans for writing a book together under the title *Power and Freedom*. Although most of Sartre's friends found this idea ridiculous and believed that Lévy was taking advantage of a sick, old man, some also recognized that Lévy efforts were helping to keep Sartre alive by promising him a future, however illusory, to which he could look forward.

In March 1980, a month before Sartre's death, Lévy published a slim volume entitled *Hope Now: The 1980 Interviews* (*L'espoir de maintenant: les entretiens de 1980*, 1980). This book contains Sartre's last words on philosophical matters and two brief commentaries by Lévy. What makes *Hope Now* surprising and controversial are statements by Sartre that seem inconsistent with his earlier views or express interest in things that are decidedly new. Sartre confesses that he used the concepts of despair and anguish in his philosophy during the 1940s because they were in vogue, even though he had never experienced despair or anguish. He also admits that his account of Jewish identity in *Anti-Semite and Jew* was seriously inadequate because it overlooked the historical, metaphysical, and messianic aspects of Jewish identity. Despite his twenty-year association with Marxism, Sartre dismisses Marxism in *Hope Now* and affirms the ideals of hope, democracy, and an ethical future based on universal brotherhood. He says, for example:

> What does it mean to be human, and to be capable--along with one's neighbor, who is also a human being—of producing laws, institutions, of making oneself a citizen by means of the vote? All Marx's distinctions among superstructures are a fine bit of work, but it's utterly false because the primary relationship of individual to individual is something else, and that's what we're here to discover (Sartre and Lévy, *HN* 1996, 86).

The publication of *Hope Now* provoked intense debate, first among Sartre's friends and then among scholars. There is no reason to doubt that the words attributed to Sartre in the text of the interview are Sartre's actual words. Arlette reread the interview to Sartre before its publication "repeating word after word, as well as the whole text several times. . . . Sartre added and corrected as he wished" (Sartre and Lévy, *HN* 1996, 8). On the other hand, there is reason to wonder whether Lévy, who had changed his own views from Maoism to messianic Judaism, had pressured Sartre into saying things he did not really believe. Raymond Aron, who had for decades disagreed with Sartre on most political issues, said that the ideas expressed in the interview were far too reasonable to be Sartre's work. François Truffaut, the famous French film director, described the interview as "pure shit." Beauvoir attempted to discredit *Hope Now* by publishing *Adieux* (*La Cérémonie des adieux* 1981), in which she gave her own account of Sartre's last ten years accompanied by an edited transcript of conversations she had with Sartre in 1974.

My view is that the *Hope Now* interview is a genuine reflection of ideas that Sartre was "trying out" in response to new circumstances. Sartre was a philosopher who was always willing to "think against himself" in order to make sense out of the concrete realities that the world presented to him. I believe that at the end of his life, he did what he had so often done before: he readjusted the language and emphasis of his worldview to accommodate the world in which he found himself. This time, however, the world had shrunk rather than expanded. Blind and helpless, yet eager as always to move on to new projects, he concentrated his attention on Benny Lévy, and attempted to make sense out of the abandonment of revolutionary Marxism by Lévy and other student radicals.

Sartre died in a coma on April 15, 1980. His circulation had become so poor that his bedsores were infected with gangrene. Shortly before lapsing into consciousness, he told Beauvoir "I love you very much, my dear Castor [Beaver]" (Beauvoir 1984, 123). The hearse that carried Sartre's body from the hospital to the cemetery was followed by a crowd of about 50,000 people. The mass of people following the hearse was met by another mass of people waiting at the cemetery. Many people were standing on top of tombstones. The crowd had to be pushed back in order to get the coffin out of the hearse. There was no speech or ceremony. Beauvoir asked for a chair and sat at the open grave for about ten minutes. A few days later, Sartre's body was removed from the grave and cremated.

Since Sartre left no will, his adopted daughter Arlette received legal rights over everything he had written, including his letters to Beauvoir. When Arlette refused to give Beauvoir permission to publish Sartre's letters, Beauvoir published them without her permission. Beauvoir died six years after Sartre on April 14, 1986.

3
Perception and Reality

A. Sartre's Defense of Direct Realism

1. Sartre's Direct Realism

Although Sartre changed his ideas about many things over the course of his career as a writer and philosopher, he never changed his common sense belief in the independent existence of physical objects. Sartre, like most people, believed physical objects have a reality which is not dependent on their being perceived. He believed, for example, that the tree outside his apartment window would continue to exist even if no conscious being in the universe happened to be perceiving that tree. He also believed, like most people, that our perceptions of physical objects put us in direct touch with physical objects and show us quite reliably what those objects really look like, feel like, smell like, etc. These two beliefs form the basis for a philosophical position known as direct realism. Although Sartre rejects both "realism and idealism" in *Being and Nothingness*, he seems to equate realism with causal or representative realism. (I will explain causal or representative realism shortly.) Despite his discomfort with the word 'realism,' Sartre was a direct realist.

Sartre was not, however, a naïve realist. Naïve realists share the defining beliefs of direct realism, but they make no distinction between what our perceptions of physical objects show us and the intrinsic properties of those objects. According to the naïve realist, the gray-green color I see when I look at a shirt simply *is* the color of that shirt. But naïve realism leads to obvious inconsistencies. If that shirt looks gray-green to me, and gray-blue to you, which one of us sees the shirt's true color? Sartre would say that in one sense both of us see the shirt's true color, since the shirt shows itself to my eyes as gray-green and to your eyes as gray-blue. But he would add that human societies (including scientific societies) select observation under some conditions as true and under others as deficient. Consequently, the gray-blue you see with your normal human eyes may meet society's standard of "true color" better than the gray-green I see with my slightly abnormal eyes. Since naïve realism does not leave room for such distinctions, it is probably impossible to make a good case for naïve realism. Even direct realism is not easy to defend as a philosophical position.

2. *Philosophical Challenges to Direct Realism*

From a non-philosophical point of view, it might seem that direct realism is so obviously right that no one could seriously disagree with it, but that is far from true. Many philosophers have argued against direct realism and drawn different conclusions about the independence of physical objects and the reliability of human perception. To understand why Sartre labored to defend direct realism in his phenomenological essays, in his novel *Nasuea,* and in *Being and Nothingness,* it is essential to know something about the challenges of other philosophers to direct realism.

Sartre, like all French philosophy students of his generation, was schooled in the thought of René Descartes (1596-1650). Descartes, who is sometimes called "the father of Modern Philosophy," tried to show that all we can ever know *directly* is what is in our minds. He argued in the following way: When I think I see a tree, I know with certainty that is what I think. I may be mistaken about what is really in front me—I may be dreaming or hallucinating—but I know directly and unmistakably what is in my mind. According to Descartes, perceptions are ideas in our minds and it is by no means obvious that our perceptions correspond to realities outside of our minds. When we dream, Descartes reasons, we think that we see and hear all kinds of things, and yet none of those things are really being seen or heard. The chestnut tree in my dream is no more real than the shrieking witch standing next to it. Descartes believed in the independent existence of physical objects, but he did not believe that perception put us in direct touch with physical objects or gave us reliable knowledge about them.

42

In a similar vein, the English philosopher, John Locke (1623-1704), argued that physical objects should be thought of as the cause of our perceptions. Locke believed that physical objects were probably made up of atoms in motion and very different from our common sense picture of them. He distinguished between the "primary qualities" of solidity, extension, shape, and motion, which must belong to all bodies and "secondary qualities" such as color, warmth, taste, and smell which were subjective effects caused by the powers of those bodies. Both Descartes and Locke concluded that perceptions were ideas which imperfectly represented the objects that caused them. Descartes and Locke were representative realists.

Representative realism is a more cautious position than direct realism, yet even representative realism came under heavy attack from other philosophers. The Anglo-Irish philosopher George Berkeley (1685-1753) argued that there was no way that one could prove the independent existence of physical objects and no need to do so. According to Berkeley, all of the qualities of physical objects, primary as well as secondary, are inconceivable apart from actual or possible perceptions of them. Qualities such as size and shape, as well as qualities such as color and our taste, cannot even be imagined except in terms of some perceptual process such as visual inspection, measurement, etc. Thus, Berkeley concludes that the reality of physical objects consists solely in their "being perceived." Of course, Berkeley still had to deal with questions about the origin, continuity, and commonality of our perceptions of physical objects. Why do I experience a particular tree in the forest as having a very distinctive set of qualities? Why do those qualities remain practically the same when I see that tree days later? Why do you experience essentially the same qualities as I do when you perceive that tree? To answer these questions, Berkeley put forth the theory that God is the source of our external perceptions and it is He who maintains their continuity and commonality. Berkeley called himself an immaterialist but he is also known as a subjective idealist.

After Berkeley, idealism and related theories took many forms. David Hume (1711-1776) agreed that there was no way to prove the independent existence of physical objects but argued that the same was true of God and even of human minds. According to Hume, we have an irresistible tendency to *believe* in the independent reality of physical objects when we are not thinking philosophically, but all that we can ever *know* to exist are our own "impressions and ideas." This view is called phenomenalism. Immanuel Kant (1724-1804) believed that there was an independent reality (things-in-themselves) beyond the bounds of sense experience, but that we could never know directly or reliably infer anything about that reality from our sense experience. Kant called his position critical or transcendental idealism. G. W. Hegel (1770-1831) crafted a theory of dialectical idealism in which the entire universe of mind and ideas unfolds over time. For Hegel, consciousness and the objects of consciousness, nature and spirit, and even man and God are but aspects of a single unfolding reality.

3. Direct Realism in Nausea

During Sartre's apprenticeship as a philosopher the dominant theories in France about perception and physical objects were some variation on idealism, phenomenalism, or representative realism. Yet none of these positions satisfied Sartre. A direct realist by disposition, he sought for ways to defend direct realism philosophically. As noted in Chapter 2, Sartre's critical breakthrough came through his study of phenomenology in 1933, but his use of phenomenology to defend direct realism overlapped with his plan to defend direct realism through description of a more literary kind.

In the novel *Nausea*, Sartre attempts to defend and explain direct realism by supposing that there is a special kind of consciousness that could reveal physical objects in a way that would leave no doubt about the utter independence of their existence. He calls this special kind of consciousness "Nausea" ("*la Nausée*"), but it is clear that this nausea with a capital "N" is quite different from the nausea we experience from an upset stomach or the presence of something nauseating like vomit. Like ordinary nausea, the Nausea that Sartre describes involves feelings of disgust, repugnance, and exhaustion, but it also involves a revelation of the overabundance, contingency, and absurdity, of the existence of physical reality.

Following Beauvoir's suggestion, Sartre incorporated his account of Nausea into a full-fledged story. *Nausea* is a novel in diary form that tells the story of the philosophical education of a (fictional) thirty-year old historian named Antoine Roquentin. In this case, however, his education is gained from direct experience and reflection on that experience rather than from the study of what philosophers have said. Over a period of about thirty days during the winter of 1932, Roquentin's view of the world and his own place in that world is transformed by a series of extraordinary experiences of very ordinary things. One strand in this series is his experience of Nausea.

Roquentin's first bouts of Nausea are relatively mild. He finds that ordinary physical objects, like the table in his favorite café and the glass of beer he is drinking, have a strangeness about them, a vaguely unpleasant and obtrusive aspect. Instead just being *what* they are "a table," "a glass of beer," they seem to call attention to the fact *that* they are. Gradually, Roquentin's bouts of Nausea become more intense and disturbing. The climax of Roquentin's Nausea occurs in a park in front of a chestnut tree, where he finds himself engulfed and paralyzed by a revelation of the naked being of the physical world.

> And then all of sudden, there it was, clear as day; existence had suddenly unveiled itself. It had lost the harmless look of an abstract category: it was the very paste of things, this root was kneaded into existence. Or rather, the root, the park gates, the bench, the sparse grass, all that had vanished: the diversity of things, their individuality, was only an appearance, a veneer. This veneer had melted, leaving soft monstrous masses, all is disorder—naked, in a frightful obscene nakedness (Sartre, *N* 1964, 127).

Without losing the literary texture of his work, Sartre manages to weave an impressive array of philosophical ideas into the twelve-page account that Roquentin gives of his experience in the park. One key idea is the distinction between what a physical object is *for us* and what it is *in-itself*. *For us*, a glass of beer is an instrumental object, an object whose properties have meaning relative to our standards and uses. The golden color of the beer, its alcoholic content, the heft of the glass, etc. are understood by us in terms of our expectations and intentions. *For us*, it is also an object with a history—perhaps, a glass that was manufactured last year; a draft that the waiter poured five minutes ago; a new brand of beer. *In-itself*, however, the glass of beer has no connection to any human concept, standard, expectation, or intention. The glass of beer *is* (it exists) and *is what it is*.

One of the key terms that Roquentin uses to help explain his experience in the park is the French expression *de trop*. Although this expression does not have a precise equivalent in English, its meaning can be translated in different contexts by expressions such as 'too much,' 'in excess,' 'in the way." As used in *Nausea*, what *de trop* suggests is the sheer overabundance and inexhaustibility of physical existence. Normally, we manage to keep physical object "in their place" and pay only as much attention to them as our needs require. If I am buying an antique beer stein, I may inspect it carefully for imperfections, trademarks, and appropriate signs of age. If I am drinking a mug of beer in a bar, I am unlikely to pay attention to any of those details. But every beer mug has such details and a great many more. No matter how carefully we examine a physical object, we can never exhaust the perceptions we can have of it.

The term contingency (*la contingence*), which also figures in Roquentin's explanation of his experience in the park, was Sartre's covering term for the philosophical content of the novel as a whole. The contingency of physical existence is only one of the several kinds of contingency that are examined in *Nausea*. What is contingency? In philosophy, the word contingent usually means something that is not necessary. If I happen to draw a circle that has a diameter of two inches, the fact that that circle now has a two-inch diameter is contingent. On the other hand, the ratio of that circle's diameter to its circumference is not contingent, it is necessary: it must be π times the diameter. One of the discoveries Roquentin makes is that the entire physical universe and every object in it exist contingently. Some objects (stars for example) may exist for a very long time, but no physical object exists necessarily. "Every existing thing," he concludes, "is born without reason, prolongs itself out of weakness and dies by chance" (Sartre, *N* 1964, 131).

Roquentin also uses the term absurdity (*l'absurdité*) to express his conviction that there is no way that the existence of physical objects can ever be fully explained. At one point Roquentin says:

> I believe there are people who have understood this [the contingency of the universe]. Only they tried to overcome this contingency by inventing a necessary, causal being. But no necessary being can explain existence: contingency is not a delusion . . . it is the absolute (Sartre, *N* 1964, 130).

The "people" Roquentin is talking about are philosophers, like G. W. Leibniz (1646-1716) who tried to prove the existence of God from the contingency of the physical universe. The question Leibniz posed is this: Why is there something rather nothing at all? Leibniz acknowledged that the physical universe was contingent, but assumed as self-evident the Principle of Sufficient Reason. According to this principle there is a sufficient reason or cause for everything that exists or happens. But how can we explain the physical universe as a whole? Since the physical universe does not *have to* exist, since it is not its own cause, its existence is not self-explanatory. Consequently, the explanation for the existence of the physical world must lie outside this world. It might, for example, be an earlier universe, but then the existence of that universe would need to be explained as well. How do we arrive at a final explanation and satisfy the Principle of Sufficient Reason? According to Leibniz, the only way is by concluding that our universe is ultimately the product of a cause (or creator) who is a necessary being. Since a necessary being *has* to exist, since its non-existence is impossible, since it is its own cause, no further explanation is needed. The skeptic says, "if God created the universe, who created God?" Leibniz answers: when we understand that God must be a necessary being this question disappears. God is his own cause, or to use the original Latin He is *ens causa sui* (a being who causes himself).

Although many philosophers have criticized Leibniz's reasoning and similar contingency arguments, Sartre's position is unusual. He rejects Leibniz's conclusion but agrees with Leibniz that without a necessary being to explain contingent existence, the physical universe would be absurd. But that is Sartre's point, it is absurd! The existence of the physical universe does not make sense, it cannot be explained. It is a raw unintelligible fact, a pure contingency.

The version of direct realism that Sartre's develops in *Nausea* is remarkably rich and interesting. But the critical question remains: Does Sartre *succeed* in defending it? The answer to this question is yes and no. Insofar as his defense depends on presenting his version of direct realism as a coherent theory the answer is yes. Insofar as his defense depends on demonstrating that there is a unique kind of consciousness that reveals the truth of direct realism, the answer is no. For Roquentin, the key to discovering the truth of direct realism is Nausea. His bouts of Nausea give him direct access to the independent existence of physical objects, and by extension to the physical universe as a whole. But Roquentin is a fictional character, and what is true for him may not be true for us. Jonathan Harker in Bram Stoker's novel *Dracula* has direct and extensive experience with vampires; he would be foolish not to believe in their existence. We, on the other hand, have no evidence of vampires and would be foolish to believe in their existence. A similar question can be asked about the experience called Nausea. Does this kind of revelatory experience exist? Do real people ever have it? Surprisingly, Sartre had little reason to think so.

In *Being and Nothingness*, Sartre returned to the idea of Nausea as a revelatory experience of physical existence, but restricted it to a modest consciousness of one's own physical embodiment.

> This perpetual apprehension on the part of my for-itself [consciousness] of an *insipid* taste which I cannot place,

47

which accompanies me even in my efforts to get away from it, and which is my taste—this is what we have described elsewhere under the name of Nausea. (Sartre, *BN* 1956, 338).

Years later, Sartre admitted the following:

What I described in the novel is not something that I actually experienced myself. For example, in the novel you see a character who does in fact possess a certain form of intuition nausea, he perceives what being is. . . . But I never experienced this nausea, properly speaking; that is I do claim it, but in a much more philosophical way. . . . But to get this notion across to the reader I had to garb it in a more romantic form, turn it into an adventure. . . . What I am saying is that I never experienced Nausea in the way Roquentin does, which is why I needed to give it the novel form. The fact of the matter is, the idea wasn't really solid enough in my mind for me to write a philosophical tome about it; it was still fairly vague, but nonetheless, I was obsessed by it (Sartre, *SBH* 1978, 41).

4. Sartre's Phenomenological Defense of Direct Realism

By the time *Nausea* was published in 1938, Sartre was already well on his way to a new and better defense of direct realism based on his interpretation of phenomenological principles and practices. This defense takes three distinct forms. For convenience, I will call these forms: a. The Argument from Intentionality; b. The Argument from Self-Consciousness and the Imagination; and, c. The Argument from Bodily Perspective.

The Argument from Intentionality.

The foundation of Sartre's phenomenological defense of direct realism was a model of the mind derived from Husserl and presented in his earliest phenomenological essays. The key to that model is the principle that what is properly called "the mind," namely consciousness, has nothing in it. For Sartre, it is always a mistake to talk about "ideas in the mind." The mind is not a container that can hold things like ideas, impressions, or images. It is not a mental substance with its own internal contents. In effect, he takes Husserl's

48

principle of intentionality, the principle that consciousness is always consciousness of something, and interprets it to mean that consciousness is always conscious of things other than itself.

In the Introduction to *Being and Nothingness*, Sartre uses this principle as the basis for what he labels his "ontological proof. " This label is a minor example of the way that employs theological concepts to explain ideas in his own atheistic philosophy. It may be worth taking a moment to consider the meaning of this label. The word 'ontology' means 'the study of being,' and the word 'ontological' means 'pertaining to the study of being.' When I ask, for example, "What do all existing things have in common?" or "What is the difference between being a body and being a mind?" I am asking ontological questions. In the 11th century, a Piedmontese monk named Anselm (eventually St. Anselm), who served as Prior of a monastery in France and later as Archbishop of Canterbury, invented a clever proof for the existence of God. This proof later became known as the "ontological proof" (or "ontological argument") and has attracted famous defenders and critics over the centuries. What this proof claims to show is that the existence of a supremely perfect being can be deduced from a correct formulation of the essence (or nature) of a supremely perfect being. Of course, Sartre's ontological proof is not about God, but it parallels its theological namesake in this respect: given a correct interpretation of the existence of consciousness as consciousness of objects whose essence, "appearing," is fundamentally different from the essence of consciousness, "awareness of appearing," it follows that the objects of consciousness must have a different and independent existence.

In other words, Sartre's ontological proof is an attempt to show that one can infer the independent existence of physical reality from a "correct" understanding of the existence of consciousness. How do we know that consciousness exists? As Descartes pointed out, I cannot doubt the existence of my own consciousness. But is it possible to get from knowledge of my own consciousness to knowledge of a being other than consciousness? Descartes had to prove God first and then appeal to God's goodness to guarantee the independent existence of a physical universe, but Sartre claims that this existence follows directly from a correct understanding of the nature of consciousness.

> Consciousness is consciousness of something. This means
> ... that consciousness is born supported by a being that is not
> itself. This is what we call the ontological proof. ... To say
> consciousness is consciousness of something means for that

consciousness there is no being outside that precise obligation to be a revealing intuition of something—i.e. of a transcendent being. . . .[or] that it must produce itself as a revealed-revelation of a being which it is not it and which gives itself as already existing when consciousness reveals it (Sartre *BN* 1956, lxi-lxii).

Stated in the simplest terms, Sartre's "proof" has this form:

1. If consciousness exists, then it exists as consciousness of a being other than itself. (Sartre's interpretation of intentionality.)
2. Consciousness exists. (Known directly.)

Therefore, consciousness exists as consciousness of a being other than itself.

Of course, the success of this proof depends on the correctness of Sartre's interpretation of the intentionality of consciousness. If the first premise is false, then the proof is not sound. Another difficulty is Sartre's assumption that the being "other than itself" of which consciousness is conscious is the being of physical objects rather than some other, more mysterious kind of being.

The Argument from Self-Consciousness and the Imagination.

No less important than Sartre's interpretation of intentionality is his interpretation of self-consciousness. Descartes had claimed as self-evident the principle that we always know . what we think. According to Descartes, I may not know whether the pool of water I think I see is really a pool of water, an optical illusion, a hallucination, or part of a dream, but I know that I think that I see a pool of water. Sartre agrees with Descartes that consciousness must always be conscious of itself, since a consciousness that was unconscious of itself would be a contradiction. However Sartre disagrees with Descartes and those who follow Descartes on two critical points.

First, Sartre maintains that the spontaneous self-consciousness that is necessary to every act of consciousness is "non-positional" and "non-cognitive." By "non-positional," he means that consciousness does not focus on itself as an object. By "non-cognitive" he means that the awareness involved falls short of knowledge. Consider, for example, an activity like driving a car. When you first learned to drive a car you had to concentrate on what you were doing (turning, shifting, braking, etc.), but as you became more experienced you no longer needed to focus on each of the many acts that make up driving. It became automatic. Now when you drive, your consciousness of driving is normally non-positional and non-cognitive. When you turn the steering wheel to adjust to the curve in the road you are conscious of turning the wheel. If someone asks you why you are turning the wheel, you have no difficulty responding. But if no one asks, then you do not focus on that turning as an object of your attention or register it as knowledge. In other words, your awareness remains pre-reflective.

Second, Sartre maintains that the spontaneous self-consciousness that is necessary to every act of consciousness includes awareness of the kind of consciousness that is taking place. Often, he expresses this through the formula "consciousness of being is the being of consciousness (Sartre, *BN* 1956, 31). " He applies this, for example, to the difference between perceiving and imagining. He claims that when we perceive an object we are aware that we are perceiving an object, and when we imagine an object we are aware that we are imagining an object. By making this claim, he challenges one of the most important arguments against direct realism, the argument that we cannot always tell what is imaginary from what is real. Contrary to most philosophers, he insists that we are always aware of the difference, even though we do not always reflect on it and register it as knowledge.

In his two books on imagination, Sartre uses phenomenological methods to develop a very detailed description of the essential differences between imagination and perception. When I perceive a wolf I am conscious of that wolf as present, when I imagine a wolf I am conscious of that imaginary wolf as absent or non-existent. Neither wolf is *in* consciousness, but the real wolf, unlike the imaginary wolf, does not depend on my whim.

To imagine a wolf is to make oneself conscious of a wolf by means of an image. The material of the image may be drawn from relatively random patterns in one's visual field—clouds, flames, coffee grinds, splatter designs, etc.—or from inner sensations—muscular contractions, internal speech, phosphenes, etc. (Phosphenes are sensations of light caused by mechanical or electrical stimulation of the retina, rather than normal stimulation by light waves. To experience phosphenes, close your eyes and press gently on your closed lids.)

Yet the content of images is typically impoverished. A real wolf presents itself to me in inexhaustible detail. The hairs on its body, although exact in number, are far more than my eyes can count. An imaginary wolf, on the other hand, has only as much detail as I give it. The hairs on its body cannot be counted at all because their number is indefinite. Nevertheless, when I imagine a wolf I know with certainty *what* that imaginary object is supposed to be. I am certain about its identity, whether or not it looks much like a wolf, because that is what I *chose* to imagine. (The same is true when a draw I sketch of Abraham Lincoln. However, bad the drawing may be it still my sketch *of* Lincoln.). In the case of the real wolf, however, my identification is only probable. That animal I see in the bushes might turn out to be a wild dog or a coyote.

Sartre's account of the differences between perceiving and imagining is a brilliant exercise in phenomenology, but does it fully answer the challenge raised against direct realism? Is there not a familiar case in which sane human beings usually mistake imaginary objects for real objects? In *The Psychology of Imagination*, Sartre deals with the case of dreams and the challenge that dreams may pose for direct realism. In fact, he begins his section on dreams by quoting a famous passage from Descartes' *Meditations*.

> I must always consider that I am man and that consequently I am in the habit of sleeping and representing in my dreams the same things, or very similar things, which I experience when awake. How often have I thought during the night of being in that place, that I was dressed, that I was close to the fire, whereas I was lying naked in my bed. It now seems obvious that it is not with sleeping eyes that I am looking at this paper, that this head I am shaking is not drowsy; that it is deliberately and purposefully that I stretch this hand and that I feel it: what happens in sleep is not at all as clear, as distinct as all this. But in thinking of it carefully, I recall being often deceived during sleep by similar illusions, and, in pausing at this thought, I see very clearly that there are no certain indications by which it is possible to distinguish clearly the wakeful from the sleeping state, that I am completely astonished by it; and my astonishment is such as to almost persuade me that I am asleep (Sartre, *PI* 1965, 231).

If Descartes is right in claiming that a dreamer mistakes the objects imagined in a dream for objects of perception, then Sartre is wrong in claiming that whenever we imagine an object we are aware that we are imagining an object. "And if this is so," says Sartre, "is not [my] theory of the image not likely to fall completely apart (Sartre, *PI*, 1965, 231)?"

Sartre's answer to Descartes' challenge has several parts. To begin with, he notes that, whatever may happen in dreams, Descartes is wrong to suggest that we can "almost persuade" ourselves that we are dreaming when we are awake. We might pretend for a moment that we are dreaming, but that pretense does not fool us. Can you "almost persuade" yourself that the book you are now reading is a dreamed book? No, says Sartre, as long as you are perceiving you cannot seriously doubt that you are perceiving.

With regard to dreams themselves, Sartre argues that the common experience of failing to recognize a dream as a dream does not result from *mistaken* judgment but, rather, from the *absence* of judgment. Dreams have the remarkable, and sometime frightening, capacity to hold our attention *spellbound*. It is precisely because the dreamer does not reflect on the kind of consciousness being experienced that the unreality of the dream is not explicitly recognized. Reflection reveals the dream for what it is, but momentary reflection may not be sufficient to prevent the dreamer from being "recaptured" by the dream.

Why do dreams have the capacity to "enchant" consciousness, to hold us spellbound? Sartre mentions three factors. First, dreams thrive on the minimal sensory input that occurs when we are asleep. In the absence of strong competition from external sensation, one's imagination is able to create the fragile structure of a dream world out of materials provided by internal sensations such as muscular contraction, internal speech, and phosphenes. As long as external sensations are not too intrusive, they may also be incorporated into dreams. For example, the sound of an alarm clock bell might be imagined as the pounding of a jackhammer.

Second, Sartre points out that dreams take the form of stories. Sometimes we are in the stories as active participants, and sometimes we remain outside the stories as creator/witnesses, but dreams always unfold in story form. As such, they sweep consciousness forward with a speed and continuity that discourages reflection. In this respect, dreaming is similar to reading a novel that one "cannot put down."

Third, the dream story locks consciousness into an imaginary mode where every thought becomes a new development in the unfolding fictional story. If, for example, I try to remember something from my past, what I am likely to get is a fictional memory. If I wonder in my dream how got I into this abandoned house, I will not remember falling asleep and dreaming about an abandoned house, I will make up a story—such as losing my way in the woods on a dark night—and that story will be my "memory."

Sartre concludes his account of dreams on a triumphant note:

We can conclude that the dream—contrary to Descartes—does

53

not at all occur as an apprehension of reality. On the contrary, it would lose all its sense, its own nature, if it could posit itself as real even for a moment. . . . The dream is not fiction taken for reality, it is the odyssey of a consciousness dedicated by itself, and in spite of itself, to build only an unreal world (Sartre, *PI* 1965, 254-255).

The Argument from Bodily Perspective.

However powerful Sartre's arguments from intentionality and self-consciousness may be, they do not address challenges to direct realism that are specifically directed at the objectivity and reliability of our perceptions. If direct realism is correct, then how can we account for discrepancies between the way different people perceive the same object or even the way that one person perceives the same object under different conditions? We know, for example, that food tastes different to us when we have the flu and cool water feels warm when we have been making snowballs without gloves. Furthermore, there are profound discrepancies between our everyday experience of the world and the picture of the world that science provides. What I perceive as warmth is described by physicists as the average kinetic energy of molecules. What I perceive as a solid lump of gold is described by physicists as a largely empty space occupied by an array of tiny colorless atoms that reflect light in certain wavelengths.

Sartre's response to these challenges rests on a third principle of consciousness: the principle that consciousness can exist only as embodied consciousness. The principle of embodied consciousness is prompted in part by his interpretation of intentionality. As noted above, his interpretation of intentionality implies that consciousness cannot exist except as consciousness of a being other than itself, and that being, he assumes, is the contingent being of the physical world. But if this is so, how is it possible for consciousness to exist in the midst of the physical world and to maintain contact with that world? Sartre's answer is one of the most radical elements in his philosophy. Consciousness, he asserts, would be impossible if it did not exist as particular and contingent bodies in the world, and he constructs a theory to explain this principle.

Sartre's theory of embodied consciousness is easily misunderstood because it differs both from dualistic theories that treat the mind as a non-physical substance inside the body and from materialistic theories that treat consciousness as a product of brain processes. For Sartre, consciousness is literally incarnated in the body as a whole. For example, when I eat an apple, my awareness of that apple is not merely something that happens in or through my brain. Rather, my consciousness of that apple is in my finger tips as they feel the apple's smooth skin and firm flesh; it is in my eyes which see the redness of the apple torn by the bite which I have just taken; it is in my tongue and nose which taste the tart sweetness of the juice; it is in my nose which catches the distinctive aroma of the apple; it is in my lips which sense the slight stickiness of the juice.

Sartre readily admits that the distinctive ways in which we perceive the world depend on the physiology of the human body and on the slight variations in physiology that characterize different human bodies. Although Sartre did not like to talk about animals because he did not want to deal with the problem of animal consciousness, a comparison with animals is useful here. If humans had a dog's sense of smell, or an elephant's sense of sound, or the capacity of a snake to detect variations in warmth at a distance, then our experience of the world would be quite different from what it is now. Thus, perceptual experience is relative to physiology. Sartre also admits that the ways in which we perceive at any given time depend on our locations and the conditions of perception. If I look down on railroad tracks from a helicopter they will look parallel; if I stand on the tracks and look down the line, they will appear to converge. By the same token, when I ski with amber-colored goggles the colors of what I see on the slope are noticeably different from the colors I see when I ski without goggles.

What Sartre does not admit, however, is that these variations imply that our perceptions of the world are lacking in objectivity or reliability. On the contrary, he insists that such variations are necessary to the objectivity and reliability of perception. For Sartre, perception is *necessarily contingent.* To see anything at all is to see that thing with particular organs, from a particular position in the world, and under particular conditions. To borrow Thomas Nagel's phrase, there is no such thing as "the view from nowhere." To see railroad tracks is to see them from one angle or another. When I stand on the tracks and look down the line, the appearance of convergence is the objective manifestation of my line of vision. When I look at snow through amber goggles, the amber look of the snow is an objective manifestation of the goggles I am wearing. When I run cool water over my hands after making snowballs without wearing gloves, the warmth that I feel in an objective manifestation of the difference between the temperature of my hands and the temperature of the water.

Of course, Sartre does not claim that our judgments about physical objects are always correct. A child, for example, might think that the railroad tracks come together. A pilot in a storm might mistake the sea for the sky. But erroneous inferences drawn from our perceptions do not prove that our perceptions are in error. According to Sartre, knowledge proper is "intuitive knowledge" and intuitive knowledge "is the presence of consciousness to the thing" (Sartre, *BN* 1956, 172). Our mistaken judgments about the physical world arise from inference and arguments. Therefore, Sartre believes that science is prey to errors that do not occur in perception itself. He tends to take an anti-realist or instrumentalist view of science. That is to say, he regards scientific theories as instruments for predicting observable outcomes rather than as descriptions of the way that world *really is*. As for the objectivity of scientific observation, Sartre does not regard scientific observation as inherently more objective than ordinary perceptual experience, just a different objectivity within a different frame of reference. When I must choose one frame of reference over another, then, Sartre says: "I give the name subjectivity to the objectivity which I have not chosen" (Sartre, *BN* 1956, 312).

Taken as a whole, Sartre's defense of direct realism is one of the finest and least appreciated accomplishments in his philosophy. It is also the foundation for his ontology.

4
Ontology

A. Nothingness

In the book *Being and Nothingness*, Sartre develops an elaborate and sometimes puzzling terminology for talking about different kinds of being. For example, he uses the word 'nothingness' (the French expression '*le Néant*) as a name for consciousness. He also calls human consciousness as it exists in the world "the for-itself," "lack," "freedom," "existence," "the desire to be," and "the desire to be God."

Sartre calls consciousness "nothingness" because it is through consciousness that negations of all kinds enter the world. It is consciousness that introduces the comparisons, expectations, and values which make negations arise. When we perceive an egg as fragile, a glass as empty, a motor as broken, a salary as inadequate, or a room as too cold, we are introducing negations into our experience *of* and interactions *with* the physical universe. Another example of the "nihilating" power of consciousness is the perception of absence. Sartre describes going to his friend's room and discovering that he is not there. The room is full of books, Pierre's books, but what Sartre "sees" is not only what *is* in the room but what *is not* in the room. Indeed, what stands out in the room is precisely Pierre's absence. Sartre calls these particular instances of negation "*négatités*" and claims that they are fundamental to the process by which we give structure and meaning to the world.

Sartre also argues that consciousness maintains its own identity by using negation to differentiate itself from the objects of which it is conscious. Thus, consciousness is always aware that it is *not* the object of which it is conscious, whether that object happens to be an inert physical entity or another consciousness. This is also true in more complicated ways for our own past and future selves.

When you remember something you did yesterday, perhaps something you now find embarrassing like losing your temper at the breakfast table, you are aware that you are not identical with that person who lost his (or her) temper at the breakfast table. You may have had experiences since yesterday morning that have changed your outlook—such as feelings of regret for hurting your sister's feelings. But this varies from case to case. What does not vary is that the person you were yesterday is frozen in time, whereas the person you are now is free to choose new actions and attitudes. You cannot change what you did in the past, but you can and must choose what you are doing now. Hence, there is a very important difference between the person you were yesterday, or even five minutes ago, and the person you are now. The person you were is now fixed and unchangeable, and the person you are is not. You are not the person you were, and yet you are responsible for that person. Indeed, you have to carry the weight of everything you have ever done and of everything that was ever done to you. No matter how much regret you may feel now, no matter how determined you may be not to lose your temper again, you cannot deny that it was *you* who lost your temper yesterday morning. Sartre tries to capture the strange duality of this relationship with the past by saying: "the past is not what I am but what I was and what I *have* [i.e. what I am obligated] to be" (Sartre, *BN* 1956, 116).

The same is true for our futures, but for different reasons. The future is the realm of the possible. Although I can and must choose the future that takes shape as the meaning and realization of present choices and actions, I cannot command that slightly more distant future which will be shaped by future choices and actions. When I hit a tennis ball, for example, the arc of my swing is chosen with the specific regard for the future placement of the ball. I choose a certain swing in order to drop the ball over the net and or to sweep the ball into the opposite corner near the baseline. On the other hand, when I contemplate more distant goals, I cannot impose my will on who I will become. Years ago when I was a smoker, I would promise myself from to time to time to give up smoking and had every intention of keeping that promise. Yet an hour later when I felt like cigarette, I had to make that decision over again. A past resolution may inform my choice but it will not determine it. Nonetheless, I have a profound relation to my future self since it is for the sake of that self that most my actions are undertaken. If I suffer the discomfort of giving up smoking, it is to protect the health of that person I will become. Sartre describes this duality by saying: "I am my Future in the constant perspective of the possibility of not being it" (Sartre, *BN* 1956, 129).

In spite of the fact that Sartre gives many interesting and important examples of the way in which consciousness structures the world through negations, one may still find it strange that he chose to talk about consciousness as nothingness. Why did Sartre choose such a strange way of talking? Let me suggest three additional reasons.

First, Sartre was trying to be both trendy and critical by adapting a way of talking that Heidegger had made notorious in his controversial 1929 essay "What is Metaphysics?" In that essay, Heidegger contends that nothingness (*das Nichts*) is integral to the Being of what-is and constitutes a transcendent horizon without which human existence (*Da-sein*) could understand neither what-is, what is not, nor itself. Although Sartre borrows key words and insights from Heidegger, he rejects Heidegger's strategy of placing nothingness outside the concrete world of people and physical objects. One could say that he brings nothingness—as the lens of existential understanding—down to earth.

Second, Sartre uses talk about nothingness to lay a foundation for his views on free will. One of the most important challenges to libertarian theories of free will is the claim that we can reduce free will to self-determination: that present desires and beliefs determine future choices and actions. To guard against this claim Sartre insists that one's present is always separated by nothingness from one's past and future and this separation is a condition of freedom. "In freedom," says Sartre, "the human being *is* his own past (as also his own future) in the form of nihilation" (Sartre, *BN* 1956, 29).

Third, Sartre adopts a strange way of talking about consciousness in order to emphasize how strange consciousness really is. One of the strengths of Sartre's work as a philosopher is that he took consciousness very seriously and attempted to give a full account of it without trying to reduce it to something else. In this respect, he anticipated the discovery of the 1990s that figuring out what to do with consciousness is a fundamental challenge for philosophy and cognitive science. In a 1999 review of two new books on consciousness, Colin McGinn summarized the radical implications of this discovery:

> Recently consciousness has leaped naked from the closet,
> streaking across the intellectual landscape. People are
> conscious—all of them! . . . The Nineties are to consciousness

what the Sixties were to sex. . . . But there is a price to pay for all this theoretical liberation: once consciousness is admitted as a real distinctive phenomenon in the natural world, we have to find a place for it in our scheme of things; we have to give an explanation of its nature. . . . I believe myself that the new interest in consciousness represents the next big phase in human thought about the natural world (McGinn 1999, 44).

Sartre understood the magnitude of this challenge sixty years ago and tried to meet it by talking about consciousness as nothingness.

2. Being-in-itself

In *Nausea*, Sartre used the word 'existence' to talk about the independent reality of physical objects. In *Being and Nothingness*, he prefers to use 'existence' (as well as 'nothingness' and 'being-for-itself') to talk about the kind of being that human beings have and to use the expression 'being-in-itself' (*l'être-en-soi*) to talk about the kind of being that physical objects have. Yet if these are merely changes in terminology, why does *Being and Nothingness* offer so many different descriptions of being-in-itself? And how do these descriptions fit together? Happily, the answers are relatively simple.

In a few instances, Sartre attempts to give a description of being-in-itself as it is *apart* from consciousness. In other words, he tries to tell us what would be true of the physical universe if there were no consciousness in the universe. He says that being-in-itself apart from consciousness is an undifferentiated totality about which little can be that is literally true. In *Nausea*, Sartre produced an elaborate metaphorical description of this kind of being as an endless mass of undifferentiated goo. In *Being and Nothingness*, he provides a short non-metaphorical summary of what can be said about being-in-itself apart from consciousness. He says: "Being is. Being is in-itself. Being is what it is" (Sartre, *BN* 1956, lxiv).

This sparse picture changes dramatically when we turn to descriptions of being-in-itself as revealed to consciousness. The emergence of consciousness in the midst of the undifferentiated being of the physical universe transforms the universe into an elaborately structured world. (In a sense, each person structures his or her or own world.) What kinds of descriptions can be given of being-in-itself as it appears to consciousness? All kinds! There are countless ways in which we can describe the world as it appears to us. Of course, Sartre is primarily interested in descriptions of the world that are philosophically instructive, but even that qualification allows for a wide variety of descriptions. Some of Sartre's most important descriptions of being-in-itself as it appears to consciousness have already been discussed in this chapter. Others include the relation of being-in-itself to time, free will, the dual being of the human body, the use of objects for human purposes, scarcity, and competition for material goods.

3. God

As the American logician, Willard Quine, famously noted, the problem of ontology can be expressed in three words: "What is there?" Sartre's answer is that there are fundamentally two kinds of being: being-in-itself (the being of physical objects) and being-for-itself (the being of human consciousnesses). But what, we should ask, does Sartre say about other kinds of being? What does he say about animal consciousnesses? What does he say about God? Although Sartre acknowledged that animals, even insects, have consciousnesses (Beauvoir 1984, 442), he avoided the subject of animal consciousness. On the subject of God, however, he had strong and frequently expressed views.

Sartre was an atheist. He did not believe in any kind of God or afterlife. Although he had a fairly relaxed Roman Catholic upbringing, he abandoned his religious beliefs at age eleven and never returned to them. In his 1974 interviews with Beauvoir, he describes the moment at which he became an atheist.

> My parents had rented a villa a little way out of La Rochelle . .
> . and in the morning I used to take the tram with the girls next
> door . . . who went to the girl's lycée. One day I was walking
> up and down outside their house waiting for them to get ready.
> I don't know where the thought came from or how it struck
> me, yet all at once I said to myself, "But God doesn't exist!" .
> . . It's striking to reflect that I thought this at age eleven and
> that I never asked myself the question again until today, that
> is, for sixty [sic.] years (Beauvoir 1984, 434).

This last comment is potentially misleading. While it is true that Sartre never doubted his atheistic beliefs, it is not true that he neglected to discuss the question of God's existence or the implications of answers that one might give to that question. He also used religious language and concepts to explain ideas in his own philosophy.

Why did an avowed atheist choose to use religious language and concepts? I suspect he did so for several reasons. First, he and most of his French readers had been brought up as Roman Catholics in a predominantly Roman Catholic country and, thus, shared a common religious vocabulary. Second, religious concepts, especially concepts of God, are an important strand in the history of Western philosophy, and, so he needed to utilize these concepts in order to place his own worldview in historical context. Third, he was engaged in debate with contemporary Christian thinkers like Gabriel Marcel and needed to address their criticisms.

To understand and evaluate Sartre's distinctive version of atheistic existentialism, it is useful to distinguish his, often playful, use of religious language and concepts to illustrate various ideas from his defense of specific atheistic views.

One example of Sartre's illustrative use of religious concepts is his adoption of the label 'ontological proof' as a name for his proof of direct realism. Other examples include his imaginative depictions of life after death in his film script *The Chips Are Down* and his play *No Exit*. What is clever about these depictions is that they illustrate "by contrast" some of Sartre's key ideas about the ontology of *living* human beings. In *The Chips Are Down*, the dead occupy the same world as the living, but since they lack bodies they can neither be perceived by the living nor act on the physical world. (This idea was used with ingenious twists in the 1990 film *Ghost*.) By contrast, the three dead characters in *No Exit* do not occupy the same world as the living; they are shut up in a parlor somewhere in the endless corridors of hell, where they serve as psychological torturers of each other. In this environment, they seem to think and act like living human beings. They reason, plan, talk things over, lie, confess, argue, fight, and even make love. Yet as the play unfolds, we discover that they are like the real dead in a number of interesting respects. We learn at the beginning, that they have no bodily needs: they don't require food, or sleep, or toilets. We are told at the end, that they cannot be physically injured or killed—because they are already dead. Most importantly, we discover that they are like the real dead in that they can never become anything other than what they have already been. Their essences have been fixed forever by the lives they lived on earth. Their existence in hell is only a shadow of real human existence because their futures are not open to alternative possibilities. In contrast to living human beings, who must continually reaffirm what they have previously chosen or strike out in new ways, the characters in *No Exit* can only repeat themselves. They are captives of the pasts which they forged for themselves during their lifetimes, and their captivity in hell is sealed for all eternity by their inability to change what they are. Near the end of the play when the door flies open, we see clearly that, although devils may have put these three strangers together, what will keep them together in mutual torment is not a locked door but their own lack of freedom. And the source of their torment is the inevitability of conflict between people amplified by their profound incompatibility as a trio. As Garcin, one of the damned in *No Exit*, declares: "Hell is—other people" (Sartre, *NE* 1989, 45).

Although *The Chips Are Down* and *No Exit* use imaginative depictions of the afterlife in order to illustrate ideas about real life, neither work is a critique of religious views about the afterlife or a defense of atheistic denials of life after death. However, in *Being and Nothingness*, "Existentialism is a Humanism," and elsewhere Sartre makes claims about theistic concepts of God. The most important of these is his claim that the idea (or ideal) of God is contradictory. I want to examine his argument for this claim, not only to test the claim itself, but also to illustrate a pattern of difficulties that applies general to Sartre's approach to atheism.

When Sartre says that the ideal of God is contradictory, what he really means is that a particular concept of God that he regards as especially important is contradictory. The concept he has in mind is drawn from the Western theological tradition that describes God as a conscious person who is self-caused and has an unchangeable nature (or essence). The expression Sartre uses to convey this idea is "the in-itself-for-itself," by which he means "the ideal of a consciousness which would be the foundation of its own being-in-itself" (Sartre, *BN* 1956, 566). Why is this ideal contradictory? According to Sartre, it is contradictory because being-in-itself and being-for-itself have incompatible attributes. Being-in-itself is a plenitude of being. Being-for-itself is a nihilation of being. Being-in-itself is what philosophers call a "substance": it is not dependent on anything else for its existence. Being-for-itself is not a substance; it requires being-in-itself for its existence. Being-in-itself has a fixed essence; it is what it is. Being-for-itself does not have a fixed essence; it is what it is not and is not what it is. Consequently, Sartre maintains, it is impossible for a being to be both a being-in-itself and a being-for-itself.

Taken on its own terms, Sartre's claim that the ideal of God is contradictory may seem superficially convincing, but there are deep problems with this claim. First, it depends on the identification of a particular concept of God as *the* idea of God, and many people would reject that identification. Second, it assumes that Sartre's ingenious but far-from-certain account of the being of human consciousness can be applied to divine consciousness as well. This is a risky assumption. As human beings, we have great difficulty conceiving what it might be like to have the consciousness of a dog or a cat. How, then, can anyone speak with confidence about the limitations of divine consciousness? Third, even if Sartre is right that God cannot be both in-itself and for-itself in precisely the same way, is it not possible that God is in-itself in one respect and for-itself in another. Sartre argues that a living human body is both for-itself (an embodied agent-consciousness) and in-itself (an object in the midst of the world). Why not suppose that God has a similar duality? Fourth, Sartre's claim is a claim about what is ontologically possible, or in this case, impossible. But how can he, or anyone else, speak confidently about what is possible outside human experience? Sartre's description of physical objects and human consciousness in term of being-in-itself and being-for-itself is powerful precisely because it offers us an overview of reality which makes sense of our experience of the world and consciousness. Take away that touchstone of experience, and it is difficult to see why we should find one ontological claim more convincing than another.

Yet the point is not merely that Sartre goes astray because he forgets to apply the touchstone of experience. The deeper point is that he does not have well-defined views about what philosophy can and cannot do, and consequently slides into making indefensible claims about what God cannot be or cannot do rather than taking a skeptical stand. He is too eager to duel with theism in the arena of theological reasoning and insufficiently interested in the limits of theological knowledge. He enjoys being the champion of a bold and provocative atheism, but fails to consider that his own philosophy might be better served by a well-defended agnosticism.

4. *Being-for-Others*

One of the perennial problems of modern philosophy is the problem of other minds—or, as Sartre would prefer to say, other consciousnesses. This problem can be stated as follows. Although I cannot doubt that I am conscious (that I think, perceive, desire, etc.), I do not have similar assurance about the consciousness of other people. I *assume* that the behavior of people around me is connected to their thoughts, perceptions, desires, etc. in the same way that my own behavior is connected to my thoughts, perceptions, desires, etc., but I have no way of *knowing* that is true. It is possible that other people are illusions, figments of my own imagination, ingenious androids, or lively zombies. I see what other people do and hear what they say, but I can never observe their thoughts, perceptions, desires, etc. Hence, the most I can lay claim to is an argument by analogy: since other people are essentially similar to me in the respects that I can observe (physiology and behavior), I assume that they are essentially similar in the respects I cannot observe (mental life). But since arguments by analogy are often unreliable and are particularly suspect when they cannot be tested independently, I am left with a surprisingly thin reasons for believing in something of tremendous importance to me.

Sartre's robust defense of direct realism provides ready answers to the possibility that other people are illusions or figments of one's imagination, but he does not deal with the possibility that other human beings are ingenious androids or lively zombies. Given Sartre's analysis of perception, I may be confident that the body of the person sitting next to me is as real and biologically functional as my own body, but how can I know that that body is an embodied consciousness?

Sartre answer to this question is thoughtful and distinctive. He admits that he cannot *prove* the existence of the other consciousnesses through deductive arguments and dismisses as irrelevant the merely probable conclusion afforded by the argument by analogy. He claims that human beings have a "pre-ontological comprehension" of the existence of "the Other." (Sartre uses the French indefinite noun '*autrui*' which can be translated as 'others' but is often translated as 'the Other.') This pre-ontological comprehension has nothing to do with calculations of probability, it is a matter of "factual necessity" (Sartre, *BN* 1956, 250-251). Indeed, he claims that the reflective "I think" (*cogito*) of human consciousness reveals beyond any real doubt that our being is being-for-others (*l'être-pour-l'autrui*) as well as being-for-itself. Thus, I can no more doubt the existence of other consciousnesses than I can doubt my own existence. And yet, Sartre insists that "We *encounter* the Other; we do not constitute him" (Sartre, *BN* 1956, 250). Our being-for-others, although not subject to doubt, is realized through everyday encounters with other people. As we make our way through the world, we discover at every turn and in many forms our intimate struggles with the consciousness of others.

One of the interesting features of Sartre's approach to the problem of the existence of other consciousnesses is that, unlike many 20th century philosophers, he does not bypass the problem, as Heidegger did, or attempt to dissolve the problem by showing that it rests on conceptual confusion, as some analytical philosophers have tried to do. Rather, he acknowledges that the problem is genuine and tries to find the best solution that he can. The solution he proposes is interesting for many reasons, not the least of which is his assertion that this solution applies to human consciousness but not necessarily to all consciousness. He writes:

> It would perhaps not be impossible to conceive of a For-itself which would be wholly free from all For-others and which would exist without even suspecting the possibility of being an object. But this For-itself simply would not be a "man" (Sartre, *BN* 1956, 282).

What this implies is that "our indubitable pre-ontological comprehension of being-for-others" which Sartre proposes as the basis of his solution to the problem of the existence of other consciousnesses is an inescapable feature of human consciousness rather than a necessary condition for consciousness in general. As such, it could be called an innate (inborn) disposition and an element of human nature, despite Sartre's dislike of the term 'innate' and his denial that humans have a common nature. Again, let me emphasize that Sartre's solution is not a proof *that* other consciousnesses exist, but rather an attempt to show *why* we cannot seriously doubt that they exist. While this may not be all one might wish, it is more than a clever strategy for dealing with a standard philosophical problem. It is also a thesis with profound implications for understanding what it means to *be* a human being.

Sartre's phenomenological descriptions of how our being-for-others is realized in everyday encounters with other consciousnesses are among the richest parts of *Being and Nothingness*. Although there is no way to do justice to these descriptions in a few paragraphs, I will try to summarize some of Sartre's key points in the remainder of this chapter.

The Theft of My World.

Although being-for-others is an inescapable aspect of being human, there are times when we are immersed in the objects around us and only pre-reflectively aware of ourselves. Imagine, for example, walking through a park when no one else is around. The objects in the park "organize themselves" around your presence and intentions. The statue is ahead of you, the flowerbeds to your right, the main gate behind you. Not far away is a lawn and along the edge of that lawn

66

there are benches. The bench you are planning to sit on is still at the end of the row, next to an old chestnut tree. Suddenly, you notice that someone else is in the park. You see a man pass the benches. If he were merely a physical object, you would take account of him in the same way that you would take account of a new statue in the park—you would add him to the collection of objects organized around you. But you recognize him as a man, and therefore as "an element of disintegration" in your universe.

> Everything is in place; everything still exists for me; but everything is traversed by an invisible flight and fixed in the direction of a new object . . . . we are not dealing here with the flight of the world toward nothingness or outside itself. Rather it appears that the world has a kind of drain hole in the middle of its being . . . (Sartre, *BN* 1956, 255-256).

Of course, this is not a permanent loss. One can, with effort, recover one's sense of centrality and fix the other as an object in the world. Yet, this recovery is not permanent either. Because there are others, each of us is condemned to continual competition for conscious possession of the world. Yet as frequent and basic as these competitive encounters may be, they are not for Sartre the ground floor of our encounters with the Other.

The Look (*le regard*).

According to Sartre, our competitive encounters for conscious possession of the world are grounded in the "permanent possibility" of being seen by the Other. Imagine, for a moment, that the man in the park suddenly turns and looks directly at you. How do you experience his gaze? First and foremost, you experience his gaze as recognition of "being seen." The immediate effect of his gaze is to focus your attention, not on him, but on yourself. Suddenly, you are conscious of yourself as an object in *his* field of vision, as a body in the midst of *his* world that is vulnerable to inspection. Your attention is drawn to your own appearance. You may wonder why he is looking at you and what it is about your appearance that interests him. You know *that* you are being seen by him, but you do not know *how* you look to him. You may guess at his thoughts, interests, and intentions, but you cannot experience or control them. They belong to his freedom.

Shame and Pride.

In *Being and Nothingness*, Sartre claims that we apprehend the constant features of our being through specific emotions or feelings. We apprehend free will through anguish. We apprehend embodiment through "Nausea" (an insipid taste of myself) or through physical pain or pleasure. And we apprehend our being-for-others through shame, pride, or related feelings. These emotions and feelings point to basic truths about ourselves, and, therefore, function very differently from the "strong" emotions (hate, anger, joy, sadness, etc.) which we use to falsify our view of the world through tricks of self-deception. We might call these truth-revealing emotions and feelings "existential emotions" to help distinguish them from self-deceptive emotions.

In the case of being-for-others, shame provides a particularly powerful apprehension of our vulnerability to the consciousness of others. Suppose that you are doing something vulgar, crude, or nasty, such as picking your nose or peeping through a keyhole to spy on the sexual practices of your best friend. Let us suppose that you do so in full confidence that no one can see you. But suddenly, someone is there looking at you. You are caught in the act. Here is how Sartre describes the experience of shame:

> Suddenly I realize the vulgarity of my gesture, and I am ashamed. . . . By the mere appearance of the Other, I am put in the position of passing judgment on myself as an object, for it is as an object that I appear to the Other . . . Shame is by nature *recognition.* I recognize that I *am* as the Other sees me. . . . Shame is an immediate shudder which runs through me from head to foot without any discursive preparation. . . . Nobody can be vulgar all alone (Sartre, *BN* 1956, 222)!

For Sartre, what is most important in the experience of shame is not the recognition of "doing something wrong," but the experience of seeing myself as an object—as an in-itself with a given nature, whether that nature is admirable or contemptible. Pride is another way in which I apprehend my being-for-others. "My original fall," says Sartre, "is the existence of the Other. Shame—like pride—is the apprehension of myself as a nature . . . a given attribute of this being which I am for the Other" (Sartre, *BN* 1956, 263).

The Body

As I noted earlier, one of the keys to Sartre's philosophy is his firm conviction that consciousness can only exist as a particular and contingent body in the midst of the world. But this is only part of the story. Sartre distinguishes three ontological perspectives on human bodies. The first (the body as being-for-itself) is the perspective that I have on my body apart the Other. Here my body is a center of reference, a viewpoint on the world. The second (the body-for-others) is the perspective that I take on the bodies of other (living) human beings. Here the body is an object in the midst of the world, but it is special kind of object, a psychic object, and its relation to the world is intentional rather than merely physical. When I perceive another person's body, I perceive that body "in situation." For example, I do not see the man sitting across from me in a restaurant as "a man on a chair in front of a table on which there is an open menu," I see him as "a man looking over a menu in order to order a meal." The third perspective (my body-as-known-by-others) is the perspective I take on my own body from the perspective of others. From this perspective I experience my own body as an object of shame or pride or my own body as an object for anatomical examination. Just as a physician might knead my left hand to detect an abnormality, I can use my own right hand for the same purpose. When I do so, my right hand assumes a perspective that mimics the perspective of the physician by treating my left hand as an object in the midst of the world.

5. The Point of Sartre's Ontology

Since Sartre uses so much jargon in his ontology (nothingness, being-in-itself, etc.) it easy to get the impression that he is trying to convince us that the universe is full of strange substances and powers remote from ordinary experience. Yet this impression, however understandable, is false. It is not Sartre's intention to add anything new to the universe. If his answer to the question "What is there?" seem very strange, it is not because his list of what there is contains items we have never experienced. Rather, it is because he has chosen to re-describe the familiar universe in unfamiliar terms in an effort to re-arrange our understanding of how it is put together and, thereby, provide us with novel solutions to philosophical problems like the problem of other minds and the problem of free will and determinism.

5

Free Will, Psychology and Historical Materialism

A. The Problem of Free Will and Determinism

Perhaps the most exasperating problem in philosophy is the problem of free will and determinism. It is exasperating because it is fairly easy to see that there are just three basic ways in which this problem might be solved and that none of these ways is entirely adequate to do the job/ An ideal solution to this problem would be one which provided a coherent and intuitively satisfying account of all of our relevant beliefs about choice, action, and moral responsibility and then proved that that account was compatible with the relevant finding of science about the causes of events.

What are our relevant beliefs about choice, action, and moral responsibility? They seem to be the following: 1) We believe that we are free to choose among the alternatives that are available to us at the time we make a choice. 2) Looking back on our past choices, we believe that (at least in some cases) we could have chosen differently even if everything else had been precisely the same. 3) We believe that all of our intentional choices and actions are based on reasons or motives. We may do things accidentally (e.g. drop a fork) without having a reason or we may do things for foolish reasons (e.g. drink too much because other people are drinking too much), but we never do

70

something intentionally for no reason at all. 4) We believe that people who are sane and know the difference between right and wrong (relative to the shared moral values of a given society or group) are morally responsible for what they do. We believe that they deserve to be praised for doing what is right and blamed for doing what is wrong.

What are the relevant findings of science about the causes of events? The natural sciences have found that the motions, changes, and interactions of physical objects above the sub-atomic level conform to precise causal regularities. Thus, a human body, no less than a sack of stones, conforms to Newtonian mechanics, and the interaction of nerve endings in the human brain conform to the laws of electrochemistry. As a matter of conviction or methodological convenience, natural scientists generally *assume* that every aspect of every physical event above the sub-atomic level is causally determined, but this is an assumption that goes beyond the actual findings of science. Sub-atomic events also conform to precise regularities, but these appear to be probabilistic rather than deterministic regularities. For example, nuclear physicists tell us that the probability of a newly formed atom of plutonium 244 undergoing spontaneous fission over the next 76 million years is precisely 50%. Social scientists have also made progress in finding probablistic regularities in human behavior. While it may not be possible to predict how a particular individual will respond to a given set of circumstances, it is sometimes possible to predict how a percentage of people in a specified group will respond to those circumstances.

The three basic ways to try to solve the problem of free will and determinism are called: hard determinism (or incompatibilism), soft determinism (or compatibilism), and libertarianism (or free-willism). Although there are many variations on these basic positions, the following generalizations apply to most variations. Hard and soft determinists agree that all of our choices and actions are causally determined by the relevant natural conditions under which they occur. But hard determinists insist that free will and moral responsibility are illusions or naïve ways of interpreting human behavior. They predict that as psychology progresses we will come to give up these mistaken beliefs, just as we have given up other pre-scientific beliefs.

Soft determinists, on the other hand, maintain that free will and moral responsibility are compatible with causal determinism. How can free will be compatible with causal determinism? According to soft determinists, free will should be interpreted as being determined by our own desires and beliefs. In other words, I exercise free will when I choose and do what I want to do rather than what someone or something else makes me do. The core problem with soft determinism is that it not compatible with the belief that we could have chosen differently even if everything else had been precisely the same. This belief (#2 above) is often called the principle of alternative possibilities. The soft determinist can grant that we could have chosen differently if our desires or beliefs had been different, but that is not the same as the principle of alternative possibilities. Furthermore, many people believe that the principle of alternative possibilities is necessary for moral responsibility. They insist that we cannot hold a person morally responsible for doing something, unless it was possible for that person—under those precise circumstances—to have chosen otherwise. Some of the most interesting arguments developed by soft determinists in recent years have been attempts to show that the principle of alternative possibilities is not necessary for moral responsibility.

Libertarianism denies that all of one's choices and actions are causally determined by the relevant natural conditions under which they occur. It claims that at least some of my choice and actions are caused (or initiated) by *me* without anything else causing me to choose or act in that way. Libertarianism, unlike any form of determinism, is clearly compatible with the principle of alternative possibilities (#2 above), yet for that very reason it may not be compatible with the belief (#3 above) that all of our deliberate choices and actions are based on reasons or motives. The difficulty is this. If it is true that I could have chosen B instead of A, even if everything else—including my reason and motives—had been precisely the same, then it would seem to be false that my actual choice of A rather than B was based on reasons and motives. Another difficulty with libertarianism is the difficulty of explaining how a person can cause choices and action without being caused to do so by something else. Scientists generally assume that every event above the sub-atomic level is caused by prior events and conditions. The libertarian view that a *person* (not an event) is the uncaused cause of choices and actions seems doubly incompatible with this scientific assumption.

B. Sartre's Theory of Free Will

Although Sartre was always a libertarian, he formulated a unique theory of libertarianism in *Being and Nothingness*, and then revised part of it in *The Critique of Dialectical Reason*. To appreciate Sartre's libertarianism, it is helpful at the outset to consider two issues of translation. First, Sartre uses the general term *'la liberté'* ('freedom') rather than *'libre-arbitre'* (*'free will'*) to explain his libertarian theory of human existence. While this use is far more common in French than in English, it is particularly useful for Sartre, since he does not believe that spontaneous acts of passion are less free than deliberate acts of will. Nevertheless, the English expression 'free will' has a well-established place in discussions of the problem of free will and determinism. Thus, depending on context, I shall sometimes use 'free will' and sometimes use 'freedom' to explain Sartre's libertarian views. The second issue of translation concerns the terms *'les motives'* (reasons) and *'les mobiles'* (motives). Although Hazel Barnes in her highly reliable translation of *Being and Nothingness* translates *'les mobiles'* as 'causes,' I agree with Anthony Manser that this translation is seriously misleading and that *'les mobiles'* is better translated as 'reasons' (Manser 1996, 118). Thus, a husband's reason (*motif*) for "accidentally" opening a letter to his wife from another man may be "to see what's in the letter" but his motive (*mobile*) for doing so is jealousy. While this may seem like a small point, it turns out to be important, since Sartre maintains that human beings freely choose both reasons and motives and yet are never *caused* to choose as they do.

In Chapter 2, we noted that in *Being and Nothingness*, Sartre defends the remarkable thesis that the being of human beings is freedom. We are now in a better position to understand that thesis. Although Sartre did not use the same terms that I am using here, he was keenly aware of the difficulty libertarians had in reconciling the principle of alternative possibilities with the conviction that all choices are based on reason and motives. His solution to this difficulty was to insist that we *choose* not only our actions and the ends (i.e. goals) of those actions but also the reasons and motives for those actions. Libertarians, he thought, defeated their own position by trying to squeeze in free will between prior motives and subsequent actions. According to Sartre, free will should never be thought of as a power that makes actions happen without prior reasons or as a power that tips the balance between motives of equal weight. Rather, the intentional nature of every act requires that it be an integral part of the complex "[reason]-intention-act-end." Similarly, the motive, the act, and the end are all constituted in a single upsurge" (Sartre, *BN* 1956, 437-438). It is freedom that makes possible that upsurge as an ensemble. For Sartre, "the indispensable and fundamental condition of all action is the freedom of the acting being" (Sartre, *BN* 1956, 436).

On one level, what Sartre is suggesting here is a very clever and perfectly logical solution. If it is true, as Sartre says, that we choose the motives for our actions as well as the actions themselves, then the difficulty mentioned above does not arise. Under Sartre's solution, to say that I could have chosen to do B rather than A even if everything else had been precisely the same means that I could have chosen the ensemble "doing B, my motive for doing B, and my intended end in doing B" rather than the ensemble "doing A, my motive for doing A, and my intended end in doing A" even if everything else had been precisely the same. In other words, Sartre believes that it is as absurd to talk about choosing an action apart from motive and end as it is to talk about an action apart from its physical execution. Thus, when we assert that "we could have done otherwise even if everything else had been precisely the same" the "everything else" cannot apply to the motives or ends of the alternative actions in question.

The drawback with Sartre's solution is that it places a tremendous burden on his theory of free will and human psychology. In particular, it requires him to defend the claim that human beings *choose* their motives. Now, this is a very difficult claim to defend. It is difficult for two reasons: 1) We assume that our motives precede our actions, and therefore cannot be chosen at the same time as our actions; 2) We believe that most of our motives (e.g. hunger, sexual desire, fear, greed, sympathy, envy, jealousy, hate, etc.) arise within us without being in any way chosen. Let us consider how Sartre deals with each of these difficulties.

How Can We Choose Motives that Precede Our Actions?

Most of us assume that our motives precede our actions, and therefore cannot be chosen at the same times as our actions. For example, the husband who was motivated by jealousy to open his wife's letter felt jealous *before* he opens the letter. Indeed, the point of saying that he was motivated by jealousy was to explain his action as a result or effect of a prior motive, just as we explain physical events in terms of antecedent (i.e. prior) conditions. But no one, including Sartre, believes that we can reach into the past and make something different than it was. How, then, is it possible to choose our motives at the same time that we choose our actions? Sartre's answer to this question is ingenious. He agrees that our motives must precede our actions, but argues that what makes them effective is our simultaneous reaffirmation or recovery of those motives in the choice we make of an act and end. Thus a husband who had no prior feeling of jealousy could not (except in one very rare case) act out of jealousy, but having prior feelings of jealousy does not *cause* a husband to open his wife's

Free Will, Psychology, and Historical Materialism

letter. What causes him to open the letter is an upsurge of his freedom which simultaneously reaffirms his prior jealousy, opens the letter, and projects himself toward the possibilities of confirming or disconfirming his jealous suspicions by what he reads in the letter. As Sartre says:

> The recovery of former motives . . . is not distinct from the project by which I assign new ends to myself and by which in light of those ends I apprehend myself as discovering a supporting [reason] in the world. Past motives, past reasons, present motives and reasons, future ends, all are organized in a indissoluble unity by the very upsurge of a freedom which is beyond reasons, motives, and ends (Sartre, *BN* 1956, 450).

What Is the Price of Choosing Otherwise?

Yet despite his ingenuity in explaining how it is possible for prior motives to be chosen, Sartre must still face an equally formidable challenge. Given the principle of alternative possibilities, it must be possible to choose actions and ends that reject rather than recover prior motives. But if we choose an action which rejects rather than recovers our prior motives, wouldn't we be acting without a motive? And if, as Sartre maintains, motives, reasons, acts, and ends always constitute an indissoluble unity, how can there be such a unity, when there is no motive? Sartre's response to this challenge is one of the most unusual theses in his philosophy. He claims that the only way that we can choose an action which (fully) rejects our prior motives is by radically transforming our original project of being and thereby adopting a new array of reasons, ends, and motives. Thus, in a sense, to change what we do, we must change what we are.

To illustrate this thesis he offers the seemingly trivial example of a man becoming fatigued while hiking on a trail and, though physically able to continue, throwing down his backpack and resting while his companions push on to end of the trail. What would it have required, Sartre asks, for him to continue hiking rather than stopping at that point? In answer to this question, he writes:

> I have yielded to fatigue, we said, and doubtless I *could have* done otherwise but *at what price?* . . . I can refuse to stop only by a radical conversion of my being-in-the-world; that is by an abrupt metamorphosis of of my initial project—i.e. by another choice of myself (See Sartre, *BN* 1956, 454).

75

The point of this example seems to be that even in trivial cases the "price" of choosing an alternative possibility, a course of action that is not based on prior motives and anchored in one's fundamental project, is a tremendous price—and a price that is rarely paid. Although Sartre is not clear on this point, such transformations (or conversions) seldom happen. Consequently, most people (after age twelve or so) never actually choose a course of action that is *not* based on prior motives and anchored in their original choice of being. Even though such momentous choices are always possible.

With respect to the free will problem, the principal advantage that Sartre reaps from this unusual thesis is it that allows him to explain why we almost never encounter examples of people making choices that (fully) reject prior motives and establish new ones. On the other hand, it requires Sartre to explain a thesis that runs counter to most people's intuitions. It requires him to explain why most people believe that they can often "choose otherwise" without transforming their entire way of being-in-the-world. And it requires him to explain why most people doubt whether it is ever possible to transform one's entire way of being-in-the-world.

With regard to the first of these issues, Sartre does not have a great deal to say. But he does point out that a fair amount of flexibility enters into one's realization of an original choice because of: 1) "indifferents" (i.e. mulitple ways of realizing the same ends and motives); 2) errors of interpretation and judgment; and, 3) voluntary decisions which are opposed to fundamental ends without really changing one's fundamental choice. To illustrate the last case, he describes a man who has chosen inferiority as his fundamental project, but who is motivated by shame and suffering (which are part of his realization of inferiority) to overcome a limitation such as stuttering. Of course, says Sartre, even if he succeeds, his project of inferiority will manifest itself in some other way.

With regard to the second issue, Sartre has a great deal to say. He not only believes that it is always possible for every human being to transform his or her entire way of being-in-the-world and all the values that depend on that. He also believes that we are always conscious of this possibility. Since, for Sartre, consciousness cannot *be* anything, say F, without being *conscious* of being F, every human being must always be conscious of being free in this radical way. As we noted before, Sartre claims that our freedom is constantly revealed to us through the emotion of anguish (*l'angoisse*). By anguish, he means the apprehension, anxiety, and sense of burden we experience when confronted with the inescapability of making a choice that will change

76

the course of our lives. (You may experience this, for example, when someone you are very fond of proposes marriage or when you have to decide where to go to college.) Yet Sartre believes that we are confronted with just such a choice at every moment of our lives. Why, then, do we so seldom experience anguish? Sartre's answer is "bad faith." We avoid anguish by deceiving ourselves into believing that we are not free, or that we are only free to make choices within the scope of our established values, ends, and motives.

The Role that Bad Faith Can Play in Any Motive

At this point, we can fully appreciate how Sartre is able to enlist his theory of bad faith in order to explain the common conviction that most of our motives arise within us without any way being chosen by us. In *The Emotions: Outline of a Theory*, he argued that strong emotions such as fear, anger, sadness, and joy are self-deceptive ways of being-in-the-world which we choose in order to avoid practical obstacles to our ends; they are attempts to "transform" the world by means of magic. In *Being and Nothingness*, he provides the basis for explaining the role that bad faith can play in our interpretation of *any* motive upon which we act.

What Sartre says about quitting hiking because of fatigue can also be applied to actions that are motivated by hunger, sexual desire, pain, loneliness, envy, pity, and thousands of other motives. Some of these, like pangs of hunger, are products of the physiology of the human body. We do not invent the physical sensations of hunger, and we cannot make these sensations disappear by an act of will. And yet we do choose at one point to act on our hunger pangs. If we are travelling, we choose at what point to stop for lunch. If we are eager to make good time, we may skip lunch altogether and postpone eating until we arrive at our destination. Bad faith enters this process when we "convince ourselves" that we cannot go another mile without getting something to eat. According to Sartre, what is true at that point is that we cannot go another mile without transforming our way of being-in-the-world.

It is also worth noting that human beings have considerable latitude in their choice of continuing behavior toward hunger. People can choose to become heavy eaters or light eaters, meat eaters or vegetarians, gourmets, gluttons, or anorexics. The ancient Romans had rooms in which to vomit after eating too much, so they could go on eating. In the Middle Ages, it was common for would-be Christian saints to mortify their flesh by fasting for weeks on end. Buddhist monks have learned to subsist on a small portion of rice each day. Hunger strikers have sometimes starved themselves to death. Where food is plentiful, all of these choices are available to us. If we believe that we could not possibly choose to acquire the habit of finding food distasteful, as anorexics do, or become gluttons who eat constantly, or starve ourselves to death for a political cause, then we are in bad faith.

This perspective on choice and bad faith also helps to lend greater credibility to Sartre's theses that freedom and responsibility have no have no limits but freedom itself. (We considered these theses in Chapter 2.)

B. Sartre's Psychology

There is no dividing line between Sartre's theory of free will and his psychology. Most of what I have said in the preceding section about Sartre's defense and explanation of free will could just as well been included under the heading of Sartre's (human) psychology. The same is true for parts of his ontology, especially his account of being-for-others. Nevertheless, I believe it will be useful at this point to fill in the portrait of the human condition that Sartre drew in his works up to and including *Being and Nothingness* with a more explicitly psychological emphasis.

Although Sartre's insistence that human beings have no nature or essence might lead one to believe that he views human beings as having no natural dispositions to act in certain ways, that is *not* his view. In fact, he believes that we are all naturally disposed to: 1) flee (futilely) the anguish of freedom and responsibility through bad faith; 2) seek (futilely) to overcome the contingency of our existence by becoming the foundation of our own being-in-itself; and, 3) strive (futilely) to assimilate, transcend, or dominate the freedom of others through concrete relations such as love, indifference, sex, and hate. Sartre does not claim that these dispositions are impossible to escape, but he does claim that they are natural, hard to escape from, and that they inevitably fail to achieve their goals. We have already considered the first disposition in sufficient detail, but more needs to be said about the second and third.

Fundamental Choice of Being: The Desire to be God

According to Sartre every desire (or motive) that a human being

78

has is an expression of that person's fundamental choice of being (*what* that person desires to be), and every fundamental choice is an expression of our common human desire to be God! The idea that human beings desire to be God—or more precisely "like God"—is at least as old as *The Bible*. In Genesis, the serpent tempts Eve by telling her that if she and Adam eat of the forbidden fruit of the Tree of Knowledge they "will become like God knowing good and evil" (Gen. 3:3). But Sartre's conception of this desire is based on his ontological concept of God as an in-itself-for-itself, a consciousness that is its own cause or foundation. He explains the connection as follows:

> The best way to conceive of the fundamental project of human reality is to say that man is the being whose project is to be God. Whatever may be the myths and rites of the religion considered, God is first "sensible to the heart of man" as the one who identifies and defines him in his ultimate and fundamental project (Sartre, *BN* 1956, 566).

What does this mean when applied to the life of a particular human being? In his biographical works, Sartre offers a number of detailed examples, but the clearest is the example of his own fundamental project. In *The Words*, he claims that the project he chose as a child— to become a writer—was not merely a decision about what he wanted to be when he grew up, but also an attempt to overcome the contingency of his birth by "convincing" himself through bad faith that he was destined to become a great writer.

> Chance had made me a man, generosity would make me a book. . . . . Viewed from the height of my tomb, my birth appeared to me as a necessary evil, as a quite provisional embodiment that prepared for my transfiguration (Sartre, *W* 1964, 193-195).

Apart from its dramatic appeal, Sartre's claim that our deepest desire as human beings is the desire to be God (i.e. to be some kind of in-itself-for-itself) has little to recommend it. There is considerable evidence to suggest that ideals, values, habits, inhibitions, phobias, etc. acquired during childhood often continue to maintain a powerful hold over adult life. But there is little evidence, I believe, to support Sartre's unitary model (a single project of being which expresses a universal human desire to be God) over pluralistic models. Even if most of the values, motives, and ends that carry us through adult life are the continuation and expression of choices made in childhood, why should we assume that those childhood choices are the branches of a single project and that single project an expression of the desire to be God?

Although it may be convenient and dramatic for Sartre to embrace a unitary model, I do not find anything in his ontology that requires him to do so. Neither does he present much in the way of empirical evidence. Even if we grant that the account he gives of his own fundamental choice of being is entirely accurate (a point disputed by many people including his mother) and a nice example of desiring to be God, it does not follow that what was true for him is true for others. To be sure, he devoted thousands of pages to the writing of biographical case studies which exemplified the unraveling of fundamental choices through existential psychoanalysis. Yet these case studies are neither extremely accurate nor terribly convincing. And even if they were convincing, the four French authors about whom he wrote (Beaudelaire, Mallarmé, Genet, and Flaubert) hardly constitute a cross section of humanity.

Concrete Relations with Others

Sartre's account of concrete relations with others turns on his recognition of the paradox of our profound interest in influencing the freedom of others. On the one hand, we are keenly interested in influencing the freedom of others, especially insofar as it concerns our own being. We want others to love us, admire us, respect us, obey us, fear us, etc. On the other hand, the freedom of the Other is not ours to command; despite our best efforts it always eludes our grasp.

In the case of love, for example, a man strives to fascinate a woman with whom he has fallen in love. He tries to capture her freedom by alienating his own. She is "the only woman in world for him," and he wants to be "the whole world for her." He does not want to possess a robot, but neither does he want to have her love as a purely free pledge. He wants to be the irresistible subject of her voluntary love. Although a relationship of this kind can be become mutual, it remains very fragile. It can be shattered internally by the objectifying gaze of either lover, or externally by the gaze of a third party.

Sartre goes on to claim that masochism, indifference, sexual desire, hate, and sadism also fail to achieve their intended results. He is equally pessimistic about the possibility of achieving a stable concord or community of freedom through the coming together of individuals as an "Us-object" or a "We-subject." He says:

80

It is therefore useless for human-reality to seek to get out of this: one must either transcend the Other or allow oneself to be transcended by him. The essence of the relations between consciousnesses is not the *Mitsein* [Heidegger's term for being-with-others]; it is conflict (Sartre, *BN* 1956, 429).

What is striking about Sartre's overall account of concrete relations with others in *Being and Nothingness* is its one-sidedness. Much of what he says may be true, but it is clearly not the whole truth. Yes, it is difficult to treat other people as subjects rather than objects and defend oneself against being reduced to an object. And, yes it is difficult to sustain a long-term partnership based on mutual respect for each other's freedom. Nevertheless, some people get very close to achieving these ideals, and most people find their greatest joys and most durable satisfaction through their relations with others.

C. Historical Materialism

While *Being and Nothingness* contains some splendid insights on the nature of the past, it says almost nothing about the causes of historical change. Had Sartre addressed that issue in *Being and Nothingness*, it seems fair to assume that his account would have been quite atomistic. Perhaps, he would have said that the course of history results from the interaction (and conflict) of individual human beings striving to realize their fundamental choices within the "facticity" (i.e. contingencies) of their respective situations. But it is hard to guess what he might have said had we pressed him with questions like the following. To what extent are the fundamental choices of being that we make as children shaped by the historical, social, and economic circumstances in which we are born and raised? Does facticity play a larger role in determining the course of history than the freedom that we as bring to bear on that facticity? To what extent do the millions of fundamental choices made by human beings at a given time and place cancel each other out in the calculus of history?

Sartre's experiences during World War II convinced him that authenticity (as opposed to bad faith), collective action, and even heroism were real possibilities for human beings. As a consequence, he came to believe that the course of history could be freely changed in unforeseeable ways by committed individuals acting in concert. In "Existentialism is a Humanism" Sartre mentions that Marxists have urged him not to rely on himself alone but to count on others, as in Russia and China, to carry on the cause of revolution after he is dead.

> To this I rejoin, first, that I will always count on my comrades-in-arms . . . in so far as they are committed, as I am, to a definite common cause . . . But I cannot count upon men whom I do not know . . . I do not know where the Russian revolution will lead. I can admire it . . . But I cannot affirm that it will necessarily lead to the triumph of the proletariat [working class]. . . Nor can I be sure that my comrades-in-arms will take up my work after my death . . . seeing that those men are free agents and will freely decide tomorrow what man is then to be. Tomorrow, after my death, some men may decide to establish Fascism, and others may be so cowardly or so slack as to let them do so (Sartre, EH 1989, 357-358).

By the time that Sartre wrote *The Critique of Dialectial Reason*, he had given up this distinctly existential view of history and replaced it with a deterministic view of history based primarily on the writings of Karl Marx. Since Marx regarded himself as a social scientist and political organizer rather than as a philosopher, he was not particularly careful about explaining his terms and methods in the way that philosophers are supposed to do. Thus, many of his ideas are open to quite different philosophical interpretations—including those of his close friend and intellectual partner Friedrich Engels. As I noted in Chapter 2, Sartre's main quarrel in *The Critique of Dialectical Reason* is with—what he takes to be—the simplistic and mechanistic interpretations of most Marxists. Nevertheless, Sartre shares with others Marxists the fundamental principles of Marx's "historical materialism."

These principles are as follows. First, the "material conditions of life" (i.e. the tools and techniques of economic production and the relations of the producers to one another) determine, at least in general, both the political and legal organization of that society and its prevailing culture and ideology. This means that the economic life of a society determines in essential respects both how power and rights are distributed in that society and the kind of morality, religion, art, and philosophy that society has. Second, significant *changes* in the material conditions of life sooner or later produce significant *changes* in both political and legal organization and in culture and ideology. Third, history progresses through the dialectic of conflict between economic classes. Division of labor in prehistoric communities led to the formation of antagonistic classes and ultimately to the emergence of societies dependent on slaves for their economic survival. These societies in turn gave way to feudal societies with lords, knights, and serfs on the land and with guild masters, journeymen, and apprentices in the towns. The overthrow of feudal societies led to the emergence of capitalist societies in which class division is simplified into those who own the means of production, the bourgeoisie, and those who work for wages, the proletariat. Marx predicted that capitalism, because of its own internal conflicts and its perfection of production technology, would eventually be replaced by a temporary dictatorship of the proletariat and the abolition of private property. In time this dictatorship would wither away leaving a free, prosperous, and classless society founded on the principle that each person will receive from society what he or she needs and will contribute to society what he or she is best able to contribute.

Is it possible to believe that individual human beings have free will and yet that the history of human societies is determined? If one means by free will Sartre's theory of freedom in situation and by historical determinism Marx's theory of historical materialism, then I believe that the answer is yes. It is possible at least in the sense of not involving a logical contradiction. But Sartre's purpose in the *Critique of Dialectical Reason* is not merely to show that these two positions do not contradict each other. Rather his purpose is to show that they complement and enrich each other. In particular, he wants to demonstrate that it is *through* the free and purposive actions (praxes) of human beings living in a world of material scarcity that the movement of history occurs. He puts it this way:

> The dialectical movement is not some powerful unitary force revealing itself behind history like the will of God. It is first and foremost a *resultant*; it is not the dialectic which forces men to live their lives in terrible contradiction; it is men as they are, dominated by necessity and scarcity and confronting one another in circumstances . . . which only dialectical reason can explain (Sartre, *CDR* 1976, 37).

Nevertheless, the obstacles to a union Sartre's existentialism and Marx's historical materialism are not all on one side. To effect this union, Sartre modifies his theories of human freedom and psychology, and, in my opinion, makes them stronger. Here are four examples.

First, he reaffirms the modification that he had introduced in

83

"Materialism and Revolution," where he recognized that the scope of one's opportunities, and not just "inner freedom," is relevant to freedom itself. Thus a slave in chains or a worker on an assembly line does not have the same freedom as a member of the middle class.

Second, he amends the rather abstract conception of human motivation that he had developed in *Being and Nothingness*. He claims that need and scarcity are the cornerstones of human life and social organization. Human beings seek to fulfill their material needs (needs for food, shelter, clothing, sex, etc.) in a world where scarcity is the rule. Thus they are compelled to struggle with nature and to compete with each other in order to meet these needs.

Third, he acknowledges that social, economic, and historical factors play a much larger role in shaping both fundamental choices and the realization of those choices than he had previously recognized.

Fourth, he affirms that purposive human activity (praxis) can be either individual, collective, or group activity and that the effective freedom of the individual can be diminished or magnified by the social units of which he is a part. The lack of solidarity in a "serial" group or class (i.e. a group with common interests but without common purpose) diminishes the freedom of its members and makes them prey to external manipulation. For example, a crowd of unemployed men competing for a limited number of jobs diminishes the freedom of each man in the crowd to demand fair wages. By contrast, the solidarity of a group-in-fusion (i. e. a group voluntarily united and organized to achieve a common purpose) increases the freedom of its members and provides a defense against external manipulation by those who hold power. For example, a strike organized by all the employees of an industry increases the freedom of each member to demand fair wages, job security, and other benefits, despite a limited number of jobs.

6
Ethics

A. Justification for Ethical Principles

As a philosopher and as a man, Sartre was deeply interested in ethical issues. Much of his time after 1945 was spent defending causes that he believed would better the lives of people who were less fortunate than himself. Although Sartre's personal life was unconventional (some might say "adolescent"), it is clear that the life choices he made were generally guided by deeply held moral preferences. Sartre prized honesty, integrity, rationality, generosity, and the promotion of freedom. He despised hypocrisy, prejudice, cruelty, and oppression. Yet despite these keen moral interests and his brilliance as a philosopher, he was never able to justify a theory of normative ethics that he found satisfactory. (From this point on I will use the word 'normative' only where it is critical to distinguish between the normative and non-normative.)

To understand Sartre's problem, it is necessary to understand how ethical theories attempt to justify ethical principles. Generally, they begin by presenting some premise(s) about what humans are, do, or desire, and then attempt to argue from that claim to conclusions about what humans *ought* to be, do, or desire. There are many different claims that can serve as the premise(s) of such an argument. Here are just a few: 1) We are rational animals who desire above all to achieve happiness and for whom human life is not possible outside of a community (Aristotle); 2) The only ends we desire for their own sake are pleasure and the avoidance of pain (Bentham); 3) We are the children of an all-knowing and all-powerful God who cares for us and has commanded us to do certain things (Judaism, Christianity, Islam); 4) We are rational agents who recognize the concept of duty (Kant); 5) We are makers and users of prescriptive judgments and principles (R.M. Hare). The first task of an ethical theory is to win our assent to the truth of the premise(s). The second is to convince us that the argument is valid. The third is to spell out the normative implications of the conclusion and deal with any problems that may arise from those implications, such as logical contradictions or deeply counter-intuitive consequences.

I believe that the main reason Sartre had such a difficult time developing an ethical theory is that his views on the human condition and especially on the natural dispositions of human beings did not give him the premises he needed to reach normative conclusions consistent with his own ethical preferences.   Consider again his view on our dispositions in *Being and Nothingness*. He tells us that we are naturally disposed to: 1) flee (futilely) the anguish of freedom and responsibility through bad faith; 2) seek (futilely) to overcome the contingency of our existence by becoming the foundation of our own being-in-itself; and, 3) strive (futilely) to assimilate, transcend, or dominate the freedom of others. It seems most improbable that anything here could be used as a positive premise for deriving Sartre's moral preferences: honesty, integrity, rationality, generosity, promotion of freedom, etc. Furthermore, his thesis that the being of human beings is freedom seems to bar him from claiming that "moral" preferences such as hypocrisy, cruelty, prejudice, oppression, or even a life of shame, degradation, and misery are less consistent with being human than their opposites. Finally, his thoroughgoing atheism and rejection of any notion of transcendent values preclude him from appealing to anything outside of the human condition.

B. Humanistic Existentialism

In *Nausea*, Roquentin, the main character, declares his contempt for humanism—in all its forms—as a hollow and hypocritical ethic. The occasion for this declaration is provided by a dreaded lunch

Ethics

with a lonely man who is trying to educate himself by reading in alphabetical order all of the books in the city library. Roquentin calls him the Self-Taught Man. In the course of their lunch, the Self-Taught Man confides to Roquentin that he became a humanist as a result of his captivity in a German prisoner-of-war camp during World War I. Through close proximity with so many men, he came to appreciate the brotherhood of men and love humanity. Although an atheist he attended Mass in the camp to experience the communion of human souls. After the war, he sought to act on his humanism by becoming a Socialist. Hearing this tale of "conversion," Roquentin tries to bide his words out of pity, but his thoughts are pure scorn:

> Is it my fault if, as he speaks, I see all the humanists I have known rise up? The so-called "left" humanist's main worry is keeping human values; he belong to no party . . . but his sympathies go with the humble. . . . He loves cats and dogs and all the higher mammals. The Communist writer has been loving men since the second Five-Year Plan; he punishes because he loves. The Catholic humanist speaks of men with a marvelous air . . . He has chosen the humanism of the angels . . . Those are the principal roles. But there are a swarm of others . . .They all hate each other: as individuals, naturally not as men. But the Self-Taught Man doesn't know it: he has them locked up inside himself like cats in a bag and they are tearing each other in pieces without his noticing it (Sartre, *N* 1964, 116-117).

It is an extraordinary irony that Sartre himself would begin his conversion to humanism in a German prisoner-war-camp during World War II impelled by feelings of kinship with other soldiers, that he would become especially friendly with priests in the camp and write a Christmas play, that he would act on his conversion to humanism by becoming a leftist activist after the war, and that he would publicly declare that his own philosophy was a form of humanism. This irony notwithstanding, the question of justification still needs to be answered. Did Sartre succeed in deriving a humanist ethic from existentialism?

At several places in *Being and Nothingness*, there are comments and footnotes that promise the possibilities of "authenticity" rather than bad faith, an ethics based on "radical conversion," and "a freedom which wills itself freedom" (Sartre, *BN* 1956, 70, 412, 627). Near the beginning of the notebooks which Sartre kept during 1947-48, he writes of *Being and Nothingness* as "an ontology before conversion" and goes on to add: "I do not deny there is a [human] nature; that is one that begins with flight and inauthenticity. But the question is whether this nature is universal or historical" (Sartre, *NFE* 1992, 6). This is a powerful question. If the natural dispositions identified in *Being and Nothingness* are historical rather universal, then two possibilities present themselves: 1) individuals may free themselves from these dispositions and achieve personal authenticity (as Kierkegaard, Nietzsche, and Heidegger suggested); or, 2) the right kind of historical change may liberate entire societies from these dispositions and establish authenticity as a new form of social life. In fact, Sartre pursues both of these possibilities. I will postpone discussion of the second possibility to the section on Ethics and Marxism.

In "Existentialism is a Humanism" Sartre attempts to justify a humanistic ethic from the standpoint of the authentic individual. In other words, he attempts to show that his ontology can support normative conclusions consistent with humanism if one gets rid of bad faith, the desire to be God, and relentless conflict in one's relations with others. He offers three arguments.

Judgments of Self-deception

First, Sartre argues that his ontology, here labeled 'existentialism,' permits criticism of moral choices based on the grounds of logic and truth. He writes:

> One can judge a man by saying that he deceives himself. Since we have defined the situation of man as one of free choice, without excuse and without help, any man who takes refuge behind the excuse of his passion or by inventing some deterministic doctrine is a deceiver. . . . I say that it also a self-deception if I choose to declare that certain values are incumbent upon me (Sartre, EH 1989, 365).

Of course, one can make such a judgment. But does a judgment of this kind have any moral force? Can one say to a person in bad faith you ought not to believe X or do Y, because X and Y are based on falsehood or logical errors. Sartre says no. If someone chooses to deceive himself, then "I reply it is not for me to judge him morally, but I define his self-deception as error" (Sartre, EH 1989, 365).

Oddly enough, Sartre may concede too much in disclaiming such judgments as moral. If the judgment is made by a person who has achieved conversion and freed herself from the snares of bad faith, then she is in a position to compare authentic existence with inauthentic existence. *If* (and this is an important "if") she finds authentic existence preferable despite the full recognition of freedom and responsibility that it requires, she may be able to say to people in bad faith you *ought* to free yourself from bad faith or at least *ought to try* living the authentic life. The choice of authenticity, unlike other choices, does not depend on one's situation and its definitive characteristics (e.g. the full recognition of freedom and responsibility) are not themselves matters of choice. Hence the authentic person can recommend authenticity as something found.

Setting Examples for the Choices of Others

Sartre also argues that whenever make a person makes a choice he is affirming one possibility over others and thereby helping to create "an image of man such as he believes he ought to be. . . . [Consequently] our responsibility is much greater than we had supposed, for it concerns mankind as a whole" (Sartre, EH 1989, 350). The normative thrust of this argument is that since others may be influenced by what they see us do, we *ought* to take responsibility for the potential influence the examples we set by our conduct may exert on others. What is interesting about this argument is that it derives its force from facts about the human condition upon which both existentialists and non-existentialists agree. The facts are these: 1) We live in a world where other people see or discover much that we do; 2) Human beings are influenced—albeit in complex and often unpredictable ways—by the examples others set.

Although this argument can be stated in a way that makes it sound, Sartre's formulation is flawed by overstatement. He says, for example, that "of all the actions a man may take in order to create himself, there is not one which is not creative, at the same time of an image of man such as he believes he ought to be" (Sartre, EH 1989, 350). But this is not true. For example, people who lie or cheat almost always hope that their actions will not be discovered and or copied by others. Virtually no one, including a dishonest person, wants to be lied to or cheated by others.

What Sartre seems to be working toward here is a principle of "universalizability," in the tradition of Immanuel Kant. Kant had argued that the essence of *duty* (doing what we ought to do rather than what our desires incline us to do) can be expressed as a "categorical imperative," meaning an unconditional command. Kant formulated this imperative in three different ways. The first formulation is: "Act only that maxim which you can at the same time wish to become a universal law." By 'maxim,' Kant meant a general rule that describes your intended action. Thus, if you are tempted to lie because it is convenient for you to do so, you must ask yourself whether you could wish that everybody acted on the maxim "lie whenever it is convenient to do so"? The answer according to Kant is no, since if everybody lied when it was convenient to do so, soon nobody would believe anybody else and lying would become impossible. Now, Kant's argument has problems of its own, but Kant clearly recognized that universalizability is a normative conclusion of his argument not a factual premise. Sartre on the other hand, suggests that universalizability is already built into our choice-making process. Thus, he is not clear on the distinction between what he thinks people actually do and what he thinks he can infer they ought to do.

Promoting and Protecting Freedom

Sartre's third argument is also poorly formulated. What he seems to want to argue is that since freedom is the being of human beings, we ought to act so as to promote and protect our own freedom and the freedom of others. But an argument of this kind requires a lot of explaining if it is to be convincing, and his explanations here leave much to be desired. For example, the kind of freedom (i.e. free will) that Sartre claims is "our being" is not something that can be increased or diminished. Although we may try to flee this freedom through bad faith and others may try to restrict our exercise of this freedom by various means, no one can make it grow or shrink or disappear as long as we are alive. Therefore, the kind of freedom that Sartre thinks we ought to promote and protect must be a different kind of freedom, not just free will. Moreover, it does not follow as a general principle that just because all human beings are a certain way, say X, that we ought to promote and protect X. All human beings are mortal, but we do not recognize a duty to promote and protect death.

Sartre's best bet for making this argument work is to take as his premise(s) not what is true of everybody but rather what is true of people who have undergone conversion and become authentic. Some of his words suggest that this is his intent. For example, he writes (and here I rely on my own translation):

> Obviously, freedom as the definition of man does not depend on others, but where there is commitment (*engagement*), I am obligated to will the freedom of others at the same time that I

will my own freedom. I cannot take my freedom as an aim unless I make that of others equally my aim. Consequently, when I recognize on the plane of total authenticity (*sur le plan d'authenticité totale*) that man is a being whose existence precedes his essence, and that he is a free being . . . I recognize that I cannot fail to will the freedom of others Thus I can . . . form judgments on those who seek to hide the total gratuitousness [contingency] of their existence and its total freedom (Sartre, *EH* 1968, 83-84).

The suggestion here is that the obligation to will the freedom of others comes, not merely from being human and therefore free, but from being authentic and therefore committed to aims chosen in full recognition of human freedom (free will).

Nevertheless, there is still something missing. If authenticity means living in full recognition of human freedom and contingency, then it is easy to see why someone who is authentic cannot engage in or approve of choices and actions which depend on a denial of human freedom and contingency. Thus, an authentic person could not support any action based on the Nazi view that Jews are an incurably demonic people incapable of choosing the good. Nor could she support a leader who claimed that his leadership was a matter of destiny, divine choice, or historical necessity. On the other hand, full recognition of human freedom and contingency need not prevent her from supporting genocide based on territorial ambition, or a factory owner who took unfair advantage of immigrant workers out of mere greed, or the oppression of a dictator who acknowledged the contingency of his position. In other words, the argument from authenticity provides some normative direction, but also leaves a good many holes. To help close these holes Sartre needs to link societal freedoms, such as political, cultural, and economic freedoms, to ontological freedom (free will) so that promoting or protecting freedom implies promoting and protecting opportunities for the exercise of freedom.

Sartre's *Notebooks for an Ethics* reinforces the suggestion in "Existentialism is a Humanism" that the basis for ethical judgment is not merely the freedom and contingency of human existence but that freedom and contingency as comprehended on the plane of authenticity. For example, he says at one point that the struggle of consciousnesses only makes sense "before conversion" and at another point how "the Hell of passions (described in B & N)" may "be transformed through conversion" (Sartre, *NE* 1992, 20, 499). On the other hand, Sartre does not forge the links between societal freedoms

91

and ontological freedom that, in my opinion, are most needed to strengthen his argument. Many pages are devoted to the analysis of oppression and yet the emphasis falls on explaining oppression in ontological terms. Halfway through the notebooks, he says: "It is not yet a question of economic and social oppression but rather of its ontological conditions" (Sartre, *NFE* 1992, 325).

C. Ethics and Marxism

We return now to Sartre's second approach to the question of whether "human nature" (i.e. our natural dispositions) are historical or universal. This is the possibility that the right kind of historical change may liberate entire societies from these dispositions and establish authenticity as a new form of social life. Near the beginning of *Notebooks for an Ethics*, Sartre makes a startling statement: "One cannot be converted alone. In other words, ethics is not possible unless everyone is ethical" (Sartre, *NFE* 1989, 9). I suspect that this statement was intended to be a question or a proposition for consideration, and yet these words express a growing current in his reflections on ethics. If, as Marx claimed, morality does not stand on its own, if ethical values are determined by material conditions, then the way to change morality is not by inventing ethical arguments and theories but by promoting revolutionary change in society. In *Notebooks for an Ethics* Sartre ponders the relationship between history and ethics and suggests that the way to achieve freedom for all may be through a classless society. He also begins to think of Marx's ideal of a classless society as a remedy for specific evils. At the end of *Anti-Semite and Jew*, a book that he published at about the same time, he asserts (without benefit of argument) that "anti-Semitism is a mythical, bourgeois representation of the class struggle" which "could not exist in a classless society" (Sartre, *AJ* 1960, 149).

The Critique of Dialectical Reason offers little in the way of reflection on ethics as such. It portrays the ongoing struggle between human endeavor (praxis*)* and the resistance of a material world that has been shaped and structured by previous human actions (which Sartre now calls the "practico-inert"). Moral values are treated as products of social and economic change; there is no examination of authenticity. Much is said about history and prehistory, but there is no extended treatment of how morality will be transformed in a classless society. In the incomplete second volume, which was not published until 1985 Sartre examines some of Stalin's policies in the Soviet Union.

Although he acknowledges the immense suffering that some of these policies caused, he attempts to defend policies such as the forced urbanization of peasants as politically justified *given the alternatives* and saves his criticism for the harshness of their execution. Interestingly, Sartre is more critical of Stalin's "neo-anti-Semitism." While he acknowledges that this policy was prompted in part by Stalin's aim of eliminating racial distinctions through integration, he criticizes the policy as implicitly racist in intent and as intensifying racist attitudes left over from pre-Soviet times. What Sartre does not examine is the significance of this example for the supposed disappearance of anti-Semitism in a classless society.

In 1964, Sartre gave a lecture at the Instituto Gramsci in Rome which returned to the concept of morality in a classless society. In that lecture he distinguished between the socially conditioned *content* of an ethical norm and its *character* as an unconditional obligation. This normative character, he says, is rooted in universal human needs and they, in turn, are rooted in human biology: "it is necessary to find at the most profound depth of human reality, that is in its very animality, in its biological character, the roots of its ethico-historical condition" (Anderson 1993, 118). But human beings, he now claims, rise above their animal needs through dependency on other human beings and their purposive actions! In other words, we become human through human culture in human societies. Nevertheless, every society that has existed to date has created divisions among people and produced alienated moralities. The ideal society, he says, has at its goal "integral humanity" or what is sometimes called "human solidarity." This can only be achieved in a classless society. In such a society, human beings will be able to fulfill their needs without being enslaved or divided. And in such a society, human beings will be able to become more fully human. In the meantime, revolutionaries need to fight against the oppression of current societies, keeping in mind that all social systems, including those that they themselves create, such as socialism, are only provisional.

Since Sartre did not publish the full text of his Rome lecture or follow it with a more polished essay, it is hard to gauge how confident he was about its conclusions. Its emphasis on the biological roots of human universality is new but not entirely so. Sartre had emphasized embodiment in *Being and Nothingness* and need in *The Critique of Dialectical Reason*. Its positive treatment of our interaction with and dependency on other human beings is very new. Does it work? Unfortunately, there is no way to know whether Sartre's rosy predictions about the realization of integral humanity in a classless society are correct or incorrect. Since no society has come close to meeting Sartre's conditions for a classless society, and since so much has yet to be learned about the influence of socio-economic structures on human behavior, one guess may be as good as another.

D. Ethics of Hope

To date, Sartre's last published words on ethics are contained in *Hope Now: the 1980 Interviews*. In his 1980 "interviews" with Benny Lévy, Sartre made a number of intriguing statements about the foundations of morality and his hopes for the future of humanity. The most surprising of these statements is his apparent repudiation of Marx's theory of morality. He says:

> All Marx's distinctions among superstructures are a fine bit of work, but it's utterly false because the primary relationship of individual to individual is something else, and that's what we're here to discover (Sartre and Lévy, *HN* 1996, 86).

Sartre's other statements are less surprising, especially in light of his 1964 Rome lecture. He speaks, for example, of "the ethical modality" (i.e. an ethical way of being) as an alternative to the desire to be God. He calls for a "pact of generosity" as a new basis for human relations and explicitly excludes both French "pseudo-democracy" and "the socio-economic relationship Marx envisaged" (Sartre and Lévy, *HN* 1996, 60), although he affirms the ideal of democracy. He also distinguishes between the hollow humanism that exists today and the true humanism that will exist in the future. The truly human has not yet been achieved. We are at present only "submen" with the potential for becoming true human beings. "We experience humanism only as what is best in us, in other words, striving to live beyond ourselves in the society of human beings" (Sartre and Lévy, *HN* 1996, 69).

Sartre also comments on the nature of ethics itself. He associates ethics with "consciousness of obligation" but also insists that "ethics is a matter of one's personal relationship to another" (Sartre and Lévy, *HN* 1996, 68-69). He admits that he overemphasized freedom in his earlier works, and now sees "the dependence of each individual on all other individuals" as central to ethics (Sartre and Lévy, *HN* 1996, 86). He adds, however, that in acting ethically one is making a free choice. He also shifts his emphasis from the idea of human equality to the idea of human fraternity—the idea that all human beings have a common

94

origin and a common end. The problem of scarcity, which played so large role in his Marxist writings, is still a major concern, but it is now treated as a parallel problem.

> So there are two approaches, and both are human but seem not to be compatible; yet we must try to live them both at the same time. There is the effort, all other conditions aside, to engender Humanity; this is the ethical relationship. And there is the struggle against scarcity (Sartre and Lévy, *HN* 1996, 86).

What are we to make of Sartre's last words on ethics? As I noted in Chapter 2, many of Sartre's friend were shocked by his statements in *Hope Now* and took them to be a distortion of Sartre's real views, caused by Sartre's feeble condition and the manipulations of Benny Lévy. I doubt that they were right, but it is hard to be sure. It should also be noted, that what Sartre expresses in *Hope Now* are ideas rather than arguments.

These issues aside, I believe the ideas themselves are, on the whole, sensible and right-minded. Here are some brief and personal reactions. I agree with him that human beings are still a long way from creating a truly just and humane world. In the last fifty years, capitalist democracies have shown themselves to be superior to Communist societies in providing a high quality of life for the majority of their citizens. Yet capitalist democracies continue to have difficulty dealing with problems of social justice. Among these problems are the chronic poverty of disadvantaged minorities, widespread poverty in underdeveloped nations, and the disproportionate consumption of resources by the world's wealthiest nations.

I welcome Sartre's emphasis on fraternity, or to use a gender-free term, ethics based on the "inclusion" of all human beings. Most of human history's worst horrors and deepest injustices have been committed on the false assumption that some human beings were intrinsically less worthy than others. Nevertheless, I think we need to take seriously the arguments of tough-minded ethicists who challenge us to think seriously about animal rights, the sanctity of human life, and the moral distribution of resources.

Although I agree that obligation to others is central to ethics, I believe this focus needs to overlap with an ethic of self-realization. It would be a shame to lose sight of the imperative of existentialism to confront our freedom and create ourselves.

BIBLIOGRAPHY
OF WORKS CITED

Anderson, Thomas C., *Sartre's Two Ethics: From Authenticity to Integral Humanism,* Chicago: Open Court, 1993.

Beauvoir, Simone de, *Adieux: A Farewell to Sartre,* tr. Patrick O'Brian, New York: Pantheon, 1984.

————. *The Force of Circumstances,* tr. Richard Howard, New York: G. P. Putnam's Sons, 1964.

————. *The Prime of Life,* tr. Peter Green, Cleveland and New York: World Publishing, 1964, reprint, Meridian Books, 1966.

Cohen-Solal, Annie, *Sartre: A Life,* tr. Anna Cancogni, New York: Pantheon, 1987.

Collins, Douglas, *Sartre as Biographer,* Cambridge: Harvard University Press, 1980.

Cranston, Maurice, *Sartre,* New York: Barnes & Noble, 1962.

Fullbrook, Edward and Kate, *Simone de Beauvoir and Jean-Paul Sartre: The Remaking of a Twentieth Century Legend,* New York: Basic Books, 1994.

Hayman, Ronald, *Sartre: A Biography,* New York: Simon and Schuster, 1987, reprint, New York: Carroll & Graf, 1992.

Heinemann, Frederick H., *Existentialism and the Modern Predicament,* New York: Harper, 1958.

Manser, Anthony. *Sartre: A Philosophic Study,* New York: Oxford University Press, 1966.

McGinn, Colin. "Can We Ever Understand Consciousness?" *The New York Review of Books,* June 10, 1999.

Nietzsche, Friedirch, *Beyond Good and Evil,* tr. Walter Kaufmann,

New York: Vintage, 1989.

Sartre, Jean-Paul, *Anti-Semite and Jew, AJ,* tr. George J. Becker, New York: Schocken Books, 1948, reprint Grove Press, 1960.

_____. *Bariona, or the Son of Thunder, B,* in Contat, Michel and Rybalka, Michel, *The Writings of Jean-Paul Sartre,* tr. Richard McCleary, (vols. 1 & 2), Evanston: Northwestern University Press, 1974.

_____. *Being and Nothingness, BN,* tr. Hazel Barnes, New York: Philosophical Library, 1956.

_____. *Between Existentialism and Marxism, BEM,* tr. John Mathews, New York: Pantheon, 1974.

_____. *Critique of Dialectical Reason, Vol. I, CDR,* tr. Alan Sheridan-Smith, London: New Left Books, 1976.

_____. *The Emotions: Outline of a Theory, E,* tr. Bernard Frechtman, New York: Philosophical Library, 1948.

_____. "Existentialism is a Humanism," EH, tr. Philip Mairet, in *Existentialism from Dostoevsky to Sartre,* ed. Walter Kaufmann, New York: Meridian, 1989.

_____. *The Family Idiot: Gustave Flaubert 1821 to 1857, FI,* tr. Carol Cosman, (vols. 1 & 2) Chicago: Chicago Univ, Press, 1981

_____. *L'existentialisme est un humanisme, EH,* Nagel, Paris, 1968.

_____ & Lévy, Benny, *Hope Now: The 1980 Interviews, HN,* Chicago: University of Chicago Press, 1996.

_____. *Nausea, N,* tr. Lloyd Alexander, New Directions, Norfolk, Connecticut, 1964.

_____. *No Exit and Three Other Plays, NE,* Alfred A. Knopf, New York, 1948, reprint Vintage International, 1989.

_____. *Notebooks for an Ethics, NFE,* tr. David Pellauer, Chicago: University of Chicago Press, 1992.

_____. "On Genocide," OG, in *Ramparts,* 6:7, February 1968.

_____. *The Psychology of Imagination, PI,* tr. anonymous, Philosophical Library, New York, 1965, reprint Citadel Press, 1965.

_____. *Sartre by Himself, SBH,* tr. Richard Seaver, a film by Alexandre Astruc & Michel Contat, New York: Urizen Books, 1978.

_____. *Search for a Method, SM,* tr. Hazel E. Barnes, New York: Alfred A. Knopf, 1963.

_____. *The Transcendence of the Ego: An Existentialist Theory of Consciousness, TE,* tr. Forrest Williams and Robert Kirkpatrick, New York: Noonday Press, 1957.

_____. *The Words, W,* tr. Bernard Frechtman, New York: George Braziller, 1964.

Simons, Margaret A. *Beauvoir and The Second Sex: Feminism, Race, and the Origins of Existentialism,* New York: Rowman & Littlefield, 1999.

Suhl, Benjamin, *Jean-Paul Sartre: The Philosopher as Literary Critic,* New York, Columbia Univ. Press, 1970.

Thompson, Kenneth and Margaret, *Sartre: Life and Works,* New York: Facts on File, New York, 1984.